Your Employment *Rights*

Michael Malone

KOGAN PAGE

First published in 1992

Apart from any fair dealing for the purposes of research or private study, or criticism or review, as permitted under the Copyright, Designs and Patents Act, 1988, this publication may only be reproduced, stored or transmitted, in any form or by any means, with the prior permissionn in writing of the publishers, or in the case of reprographic reproduction in accordance with the terms of licences issued by the Copyright Licensing Agency. Enquiries concerning reproduction outside those terms should be sent to the publishers at the undermentioned address:

Kogan Page Limited
120 Pentonville Road
London N1 9JN

© Michael Malone 1992

British Library Cataloguing in Publication Data

A CIP record for this book is available from the British Library.

ISNB 0-7494-0723-9

Printed and bound in Great Britain by Clays Ltd, St Ives plc.

Contents

Introduction — 7
1. Your Rights as a Job Applicant — 11
2. Your Right to be Paid — 21
3. Your Other Contract Rights — 27
4. Your Right to Time Off — 31
5. Your Rights if you are Pregnant — 33
6. Your Rights if you are Sick — 41
7. Your Right to Safety at Work — 43
8. Your Right to Equal Pay — 45
9. Your Right to Equal Opportunity — 49
10. Your Rights if you are Sacked — 55
11. Your Rights if you Walk Out — 71
12. Your Rights if you are Made Redundant — 79
13. Your Rights as a Trade Union Member (or Non-member) — 87
14. Your Rights as an Ex-employee — 91
15. Claiming Your Rights — 95
16. Other People's Rights Against You — 107

Index — 111

The purpose of this book is to explain in ordinary language the employment rights enjoyed by most employees. The book does not go into all the complications which can arise in individual cases, for example the effect on your employment rights of changing from full-time work to part-time work. You should therefore go to one of the places mentioned in Chapter 15 for detailed advice in the light of your individual circumstances.

Introduction

Is this book for you?

This book is mainly about the rights of employees who work in Great Britain. This immediately raises two questions:

- Are you an employee?
- Do you work in Great Britain?

Neither of these questions is as simple as it seems.

You will normally be an employee if tax and National Insurance contributions are deducted from your pay or if you work under a contract which describes you as an employee. Even if you are technically self-employed, the law may sometimes treat you as an employee for the purpose of giving you most of the employment rights described in this book, so long as your 'employer' controls the way in which you do your work. Moreover, you may have rights under the Race Relations Act, the Sex Discrimination Act and the Equal Pay Act even if you are self-employed in the true sense of the word.

What about the place where you work? There is no doubt that you work in Great Britain if you report to a factory, shop or office in Great Britain and spend all your time there or travelling within the country. The position is more complicated if your work takes you overseas. You will have most of the rights described in this book if your working base is in Great Britain, but we shall see that some rights (most importantly those relating to sex discrimination and racial discrimination) are lost if you work wholly or mainly outside Great Britain. You may be regarded as working in Great Britain if you work on an oil platform or other offshore installation in British territorial waters or on a British ship or aircraft (unless the whole of your work is out of Britain and British territorial waters or air space).

Your Employment Rights

Scotland

Most of the rights described in this book have been given to employees by Parliament or by EC law. These rights, which you can enforce through the Industrial Tribunal system described in Chapter 15, are enjoyed by employees in Scotland as well as England and Wales, although the Scottish Tribunals have separate rules of procedure.

Some of the rights described in Chapters 2, 3, 7 and 10 are common law rights, i.e. rights which have been developed by the Courts over many years. The common law rights described in these chapters apply only to employees in England and Wales. Although employees in Scotland have many broadly similar rights, Scotland has its own legal system with its own procedure and terminology.

Northern Ireland

This book is not for you if you work in Northern Ireland. You will have many rights similar to those enjoyed by employees in England, Wales and Scotland, but there are important differences. For example, Northern Ireland, unlike any other part of the United Kingdom, has laws against religious discrimination

Your job

You may not have some of the rights described in this book because of the kind of work you do. You will find that you are excluded from many rights if you are a member of the armed forces and from some if you are a civil servant. There may be special rights and alternative procedures, however, which in effect give you the equivalent of some of these rights.

Length of service

There are some rights which you will acquire only after working continuously for your employer for a specified period (two years if you are normally employed to work 16 hours or more each week). Service with a previous employer may count if the business has changed hands. Other rights, such as those relating to equal pay

Introduction

and discrimination, are enjoyed from the start of your employment.

Illegal contracts

You are likely to lose all or most of your rights if you are employed to do some illegal act or if you and your employer conspire to avoid payment of tax and National Insurance contributions on your wages.

Time limits

Most of the employment rights given to you by Parliament or by EC law are enforced through the Industrial Tribunals, not the Courts. There is a strict time limit for bringing claims. In most cases this time limit is only three months, although the time limit for claiming a redundancy payment is six months. Only in exceptional cases can the time limit be extended. If you fail to act in time you will probably lose your rights altogether.

Help with your case

It can be difficult to enforce your employment rights without help. Chapter 15 mentions some of the places where you can go for help.

Changes in the law

The law does not stand still. Parliament is always passing new laws. The law can also be changed as a result of decisions by our own Courts or the EC Courts. This book explains the law as it stood on 1 April 1992.

CHAPTER 1
Your Rights as a Job Applicant

You do not have an automatic right to be appointed to a job which you apply for, even if you are the brightest and the best of the applicants. In general, employers are free to be irrational, incompetent and slipshod in the way they go about recruiting staff.

There are, however, some important exceptions. You could have a claim against a prospective employer if he fails to employ you or give you an interview as a result of:

- Racial discrimination
- Sex discrimination
- Trade union membership
- Non-membership of a trade union.

Direct racial and sex discrimination

When you apply for a job, the law does not allow the employer to give weight to any of the following factors:

- Your sex
- The fact that you are married
- The fact that you have previously made or supported a complaint under the Sex Discrimination Act or the Equal Pay Act (and done so in good faith).

If you employer does give weight to any of these factors, this is direct discrimination under the Sex Discrimination Act and you can complain to an Industrial Tribunal.

You have a similar right, under the Race Relations Act, if the employer gives weight to any of the following matters:

- Your colour
- The ethnic group you belong to

Your Employment Rights

- The country you come from
- Your nationality
- The fact that you have previously made or supported a complaint under the Race Relations Act (and done so in good faith).

The following is a straightforward example of direct discrimination:-

> You are a man. At your local Jobcentre you see details of a job as a bar person. One of the staff at the Jobcentre telephones the public house. The licensee states that he wants a woman for the job, because the customers prefer to be served by a woman.

This is direct sex discrimination. Even though you have never met the licensee and have had no direct dealings with him, you can take your case to an Industrial Tribunal. You will almost certainly find that the Jobcentre manager will take the case seriously and will be supportive.

The following is a case which may or may not involve direct discrimination:

> You are of Indian origin, with an obviously Indian name. You apply for a post in a laboratory. You have first class qualifications for the post and ample relevant experience. You receive a polite letter of rejection, telling you that there were hundreds of applicants and that it was impossible to interview all of them.

The decision not to interview you may or may not have been because of your colour or ethnic origin. You simply have no idea, because you know nothing about the candidates who were interviewed and their qualifications. In cases such as this, where you have nothing more than a suspicion that there may have been discrimination against you, there is a useful procedure available under both the Race Relations Act and the Sex Discrimination Act. You can send a special questionnaire to the employer, asking relevant questions. In the above example the questions could include:

- What were the qualifications of each of the shortlisted candidates?
- How many ethnic minority candidates were there and how many of these candidates were interviewed?
- How many candidates were there in all and how many were interviewed?

- What criteria were used for shortlisting?
- Why was I not shortlisted?

The questionnaire can be obtained from the Commission for Racial Equality (and the Equal Opportunities Commission in sex discrimination cases). Their addresses are given in Chapter 15. You can also obtain the forms from your local Jobcentre or employment office or unemployment benefit office.

Indirect discrimination

The definition of indirect discrimination is very complicated. The exact meaning of it has been considered several times by the Courts. The definition below is a simplification, in more straightforward language, of that used in the Act. There is indirect sex discrimination against you as a woman in the following circumstances:

(a) You are ineligible for a job because there is some requirement or condition which you cannot comply with.
(b) This requirement or condition applies equally to candidates of both sexes.
(c) It tends, however, to disqualify women rather than men.
(d) The employer cannot justify it.

There are similar definitions of indirect sex discrimination against men, against married woman (as opposed to single women) and against married men (as opposed to single men). There is also a similar definition of indirect racial discrimination. Take the following example:

> You are Irish and have worked as a driver for many years, but mainly in Eire. You moved to England only a couple of years ago. You apply for a job as a van driver in England, but there is a requirement that you must have held a UK driving licence for at least three years. This requirement is discriminatory in its effect against you because of your Irish national origin. The employer would find it difficult to justify the requirement, because it should be irrelevant to your driving ability whether you have obtained your driving experience in England or in Ireland.

There is one major snag about complaining of indirect sex or racial discrimination. You will not be entitled to any compensation if the employer can prove that there was no discriminatory motive for

Your Employment Rights

the requirement or condition which you are complaining about. Suppose that in the above example the employer can satisfy the Industrial Tribunal that he was not intending to exclude candidates from Ireland or from any other overseas country. He had simply not thought about the matter. You may win your case, but you will not receive any money at the end of it.

The compensation for direct racial and sex discrimination will be considered later in this chapter. The compensation is worked out in the same way, whether you are complaining about racial or sex discrimination or discrimination on account of trade union membership or non-membership.

Exceptions

There are very few exceptional cases in which racial or sex discrimination against you is permitted. The most important exception, which applies to both kinds of discrimination, is that you have no rights when applying for a job which will involve working wholly or mainly outside Great Britain. You could, however, have rights if you apply for a job on a British ship or aircraft or on an oil platform, so long as some work in Britain or British territorial waters will be involved.

There are special rules and procedures if you wish to complain about sex discrimination against you as an applicant to join the armed forces.

You have no right to complain of racial discrimination against you as an applicant for a job in a private household; for example, as a domestic servant. Even when applying for a job in a private household, however, you have a right not to be victimised for anything which you have previously done in good faith in relation to a complaint of racial discrimination (whether making a complaint yourself or giving evidence for somebody else). There are also rules against domestic employers advertising their intention to discriminate, but a breach of these rules will not give any right of action to you personally.

There are a few cases where being a man or being a woman or belonging to some particular racial group can be what is called a 'genuine occupational qualification' for a job. This GOQ exception rarely succeeds in practice. The following are examples of jobs where the exception could apply so as to permit sex discrimination:

Your Rights as a Job Applicant

(a) Modelling or acting, where a model or actor of one sex rather than the other is required for reasons of authenticity.
(b) A job as a social worker or probation officer, involving sensitive work with clients of one sex rather than the other.
(c) Some jobs in single sex establishments, such as prisons and hospitals.
(d) A few jobs where either a man or a woman would be unsuitable on grounds of decency or privacy. These exceptions include some jobs in private households and can also include jobs such as that of lavatory attendant.
(e) Jobs which involve living on premises provided by the employer, where it is not practicable to provide separate lavatory or sleeping accommodation for employees of both sexes.
(f) Jobs designated for married couples, such as running a club or public house.
(g) A job which involves working in a foreign country where a woman would be unacceptable (such as selling goods to Arab customers).

The GOQ defence, if put forward by an employer, should not be taken at face value. Even when the job is of a kind where the exception could apply, Industrial Tribunals look carefully at the circumstances to satisfy themselves that there is no alternative course of action which a reasonable employer would adopt. The same is true of the GOQ exceptions in racial discrimination cases. These are far more limited. The following are examples of the handful of jobs where the exception could apply:

(a) A job as a waiter in an Indian or Chinese restaurant, where an Indian or Chinese waiter is required in order to create the right atmosphere.
(b) Modelling or acting, where a model or actor of a particular racial group is required for reasons of authenticity.
(c) A job as a social worker or probation officer, involving sensitive work with members of a particular racial group.

You will see that (b) and (c) above correspond to the similar GOQ exceptions under the Sex Discrimination Act. Discrimination against you is not permitted on the ground that the employer is positively discriminating in favour of members of the opposite sex or members of some ethnic minority group. While employers can

15

Your Employment Rights

encourage applications for jobs from members of an 'under represented' sex or minority group, there must be no discrimination at the point of selection for a post.

Discrimination against union members or non-members

You have the right not to be turned down for a job, or have your job application affected in any way, for any of the following reasons:

- Because you are a member of a trade union
- Because you will not resign from a union
- Because you insist on reserving the right to join a union
- Because you are not a member of a union
- Because you are unwilling to join a union
- Because you will not undertake to remain a union member.

If you are not a union member and are unwilling to join, a prospective employer cannot insist that you agree to make payments (whether to a union fund or to a charity or anywhere else) equivalent to the contributions which you would have had to pay as a union member.

If you are turned down for a job or left off the short list for any of the above reasons, you can take your case to an Industrial Tribunal and claim compensation, just as you could if you had been the victim of direct racial or sex discrimination.

Exceptions

There are a few jobs where these rights do not apply. These exceptional jobs are:

- A post as a trade union officer
- Jobs in the Navy, Army and Air Force (but not the reserve forces)
- A job as a police officer
- Any job where you would in the ordinary way work outside Great Britain
- A job as master or member of the crew of a fishing vessel, if you would be paid only by receiving a share of the profits
- Any job where a government minister certifies that the right to join a union does not apply on grounds of national security.

It may be difficult to prove that there has been discrimination on account of your trade union membership or non-membership. There is not the same questionnaire procedure as there is in racial and sex discrimination cases. Occasionally, however, the discrimination may be unconcealed; for example, where the intention to discriminate is openly admitted in the job advertisement or where the employer tells you apologetically that he will not be able to take you on as non-union member because the union would not allow it. You will also, if your case goes to an Industrial Tribunal, be entitled to require the employer to produce documents such as job applications from other candidates. If you can satisfy the Tribunal that you were the strongest candidate, this could lead to a finding in your favour unless the employer can give a satisfactory explanation.

Compensation

The rules for compensation are the same, whether you are complaining about racial or sex discrimination or discrimination against you on account of trade union membership or non-membership. The Industrial Tribunal can award compensation to cover any actual or prospective financial loss and also compensation for injured feelings. There is a maximum amount of compensation. This amount is increased every couple of years. The current maximum is £10,000.

Rights against other bodies

You have rights against employment agencies as well as employers. If an employment agency is guilty of racial or sex discrimination towards you or discriminates because you are a union member or non-member, you can take both the employer and the employment agency to an Industrial Tribunal.

You also have rights against trade unions in respect of any racial or sex discrimination against you. If you have a complaint about discrimination on the ground of non-membership of a union, any trade union which has played a part in the employer's discrimination may be joined in the proceedings and could be ordered to pay part of the compensation.

Time limits

There are strict time limits for starting proceedings for racial or sex discrimination or discrimination on account of union member-

Your Employment Rights

ship or non-membership. You must start the proceedings within three months after the act of discrimination which you are complaining about. This time limit is extended only in exceptional circumstances. It is not a good idea to wait until the three months are nearly up before you commence proceedings, because if there if some unexpected delay at that stage you could well be out of time. The procedure for starting the proceedings is explained in Chapter 15.

Help with your case

Complaints about racial or sex discrimination can be very difficult and complicated. If you believe that there has been racial discrimination against you, you should ask for advice and information from the Commission for Racial Equality. If you believe that there may have been sex discrimination against you, you should speak to the Equal Opportunities Commission. The addresses and telephone numbers of both Commissions are given in Chapter 15.

Rehabilitation of offenders

If you have been convicted of a criminal offence, the conviction may become 'spent' after a period of years. This period varies, depending on whether you were given a custodial sentence and the length of any such sentence. If the sentence was more than 30 months, the conviction never becomes spent.

If you are looking for work, and have a conviction which has become spent, you are not obliged to tell prospective employers about it. If you do tell the employer, or if he finds out for himself, he is not supposed to turn you down for the job because of the conviction. However, if he does, there is in practice nothing that you can do about it.

Disabled job applicants

Some employers, including several large and well-known companies, have sensible and enlightened policies for employing disabled people. They recognise that even serious disabilities can often be overcome by determined employees. In cases where modifications are needed to premises or equipment, these can often be made at

Your Rights as a Job Applicant

fairly modest expense and also a grant towards the cost may be available.

If, however, an employer turns you down for a job because of your disability, there is in practice very little you can do about it. Employers with 20 or more employees are supposed to meet a quota of 3 per cent of registered disabled employees, so that where an employer has 100 employees three registered disabled should be included. Employers can obtain exemption in certain circumstances, but there have been few exemptions granted. The law also specifies two jobs, as lift attendant and car park attendant, for which registered disabled applicants should be given priority. In practice most employers disregard these obligations. They can in theory be prosecuted, but few prosecutions are brought. If you, as a registered disabled person, are turned down for a job, there is no procedure for you to go to a Court or Industrial Tribunal to seek compensation, even if the employer is below quota.

CHAPTER 2
Your Right to be Paid

The amount of pay which you are to receive for your work is a matter to be agreed between you and your employer. Your pay will generally be either a weekly, monthly or yearly wage or salary or an agreed amount per hour. There may also be a rate of pay for overtime and perhaps a guaranteed amount of overtime. There could also be agreed arrangements for bonus and commission.

As a general rule, you (or your union on your behalf) are entirely free to negotiate the rate of pay. The law does not interfere. There are only two exceptions to this general rule. First, there are still some jobs covered by Wages Council Orders, so there is a fixed minimum amount of pay. Second, there are statutory requirements relating to equal pay as between men and women employed on similar work or work of equal value. These rules are explained in Chapter 8.

Deductions from pay

The law also restricts your employer's right to make any deductions from your pay. Under the Wages Act money may be deducted from your wage only if the deduction is authorised by statute or your contract or if you have expressly agreed to it. There are very few exceptions to this rule. The main ones are that your employer can make a deduction to recover an overpayment of wages or expenses and can also deduct money if you are taking part in a strike or other industrial action. Your employer can also deduct money which you have agreed in writing can be paid to a third party or money which your employer is entitled to under a Court Order or Tribunal decision.

It has in the past been common practice, in certain retail trades, for employers to deduct money from wages to make good shortages of stock or cash. Under the Wages Act, no such

Your Employment Rights

deduction may be made unless you have agreed in writing to deductions of this kind being made, either in your contract of employment or in some separate document. There are also the following rules:

(a) Before deducting any money, your employer must give you a written statement of the total amount which is due from you in respect of the shortage and a written demand for payment.
(b) The demand must be made on one of your pay days.
(c) The demand must also be made within 12 months after the date when your employer became aware, or should have become aware, of the shortage.
(d) Your employer may not deduct more than one-tenth of your gross wages for any week (except on your final pay day). If the amount which is due to your employer comes to more than one-tenth of your gross wages then the balance can be carried forward to be deducted from future wages (subject to the one-tenth limit on each pay day except the last).

Almost all employees have these rights under the Wages Act. You will only be excluded from the right if you ordinarily work outside Great Britain or (possibly) if you are a merchant seaman or a member of the armed forces.

If money is wrongly deducted, you may submit an Industrial Tribunal application within three months in order to recover the amount wrongly deducted.

Unpaid wages

These Wages Act provisions can also be used if your employer owes you wages or holiday pay. You have the choice either of suing in the County Court or taking your case to an Industrial Tribunal (so long as you do so within the three-month time limit). In practice claims for unpaid wages are usually brought after the employment has ended.

Wage reductions

Your employer is not entitled to impose a wage reduction on you, unless there is some express provision in your contract giving him the right to do so. Otherwise, if he wishes to reduce your wage, he must in effect give due notice to terminate your contract and then offer you a new contract at the reduced rate. If the new terms are

Your Right to be Paid

not acceptable to you, you can refuse to accept the new contract and bring a claim for unfair dismissal. This claim should succeed if your employer does not have reasonable grounds for seeking the wage reduction or if he has gone about the matter in an unreasonable way. Your rights relating to unfair dismissal are explained in Chapter 10.

Lay-offs and short-time working

Your employer may, in difficult economic circumstances, try to save money by laying you off for a time or by operating short-time working. In these circumstances, the first question is to find out what the position is under your contract or any relevant collective agreement.

You may well find that under the terms of your contract or the collective agreement your employer has the right to lay you off or reduce your working hours for a short time. There is likely also, however, to be an agreement by your employer to pay a guaranteed minimum wage during this period.

If your employer does not have the right to lay you off or put you on short-term working, you can either accept the position in the hope that things will improve or treat yourself as constructively dismissed (this subject is dealt with in Chapter 11). You could also sue in the Courts or complain to an Industrial Tribunal under the Wages Act to recover the difference between the wage which you actually receive and the wage which you should be paid under your contract. If you accept short-time working, there is a risk that you may after a time be regarded as having agreed to a variation of your contract, so that you are now employed for the reduced working week.

If you are laid off or put on short time for at least four consecutive weeks, you could have the right to leave your employment and claim a redundancy payment. You could have the same right if shorter spells of lay-off or short-time working add up to at least 6 weeks within a 13-week period. A lay-off means that you are not working at all and short-time working means that you are receiving less than half your usual week's pay. You cannot count any week in which the lay-off or short-time working is caused by a strike or lock out.

To claim the redundancy payment you must take the following steps:

Your Employment Rights

(a) You must give your employer written notice of your intention to claim a redundancy payment because of the lay-off or short-time working. You cannot give this notice before the last day of the four or six weeks of lay-off or short-time working. You must then make sure that your employer receives the notice within the four weeks starting with that last day.

(b) You must also give your employer notice of termination of your employment. You can give this notice at the same time as your notice of intention to claim a redundancy payment. You must in any case make sure that your employer receives the notice within four weeks after the date of your notice of intention to claim (unless in the meantime you receive the counter-notice mentioned below).

Your employer does not have to accept the position and pay up. When you give your notice of intention to claim, your employer has seven days in which to give you a counter-notice. You will then lose your right to a redundancy payment, as long as there is a reasonable prospect of a return to normal working within four weeks after the date of your notice of intention to claim. If your employer will not withdraw the counter-notice then you will have to apply to an Industrial Tribunal for a redundancy payment. The Tribunal will then decide whether you are entitled to the payment.

If your employer gives you a counter-notice and then withdraws it, you then have three weeks to give notice to terminate your employment. If your claim goes to an Industrial Tribunal, you have to give your notice of termination within three weeks after the Tribunal decision.

In order to take advantage of this right to claim a redundancy payment you must meet all the conditions which give you the right to redundancy pay if made redundant. These conditions are explained in Chapter 12. One of the most important is that you must have at least two years' continuous service at the relevant date.

Guaranteed pay

So long as you have been employed for at least one month, working normally at least 16 hours a week, you also have a right

Your Right to be Paid

to a guaranteed rate of pay for any day when your employer does not provide you with any work at all. The amount which you can claim is your average daily rate of pay, subject to a maximum of £14.10. You cannot claim for more than five days in any three-month period.

- You do not have the right if the reason for work not being provided is a strike or lock-out involving your employer (whether or not you personally are involved).
- You also lose the right if your employer offers suitable alternative work.
- You do not have the right if you ordinarily work outside Great Britain or if you are a share fisherman or in the police service.

Your employer's insolvency

If your employer is insolvent you can claim certain arrears of pay from the Redundancy Payments Office. Insolvency means bankruptcy in the case of an individual who employs you and liquidation if you are employed by a company. The amounts which you can claim are up to eight weeks' pay prior to the date when your employer became insolvent. The amount of a week's pay which you can claim is limited to a figure which is from time to time laid down by Parliament. The figure up to 31 March 1992 was £198. On 1 April 1992 the figure went up to £205.

You can also claim arrears of holiday pay for up to six weeks, so long as the holiday pay relates to the 12 months prior to your employer's insolvency.

You do not have these rights if you ordinarily work outside the EC or if you are a share fisherman or merchant seaman. Also, you do not have the right if you are a civil servant or other Crown employee, but it is to be hoped that the likelihood of your employer becoming insolvent is fairly remote in these circumstances.

CHAPTER 3
Your Other Contract Rights

It is unlikely that you will be suing your employer for breach of contract while you are still employed. Legal proceedings between you and your boss do not generally lead to a happy working relationship. Claims by you against your employer or by your employer against you are more likely to be made after the employment has come to an end.

Negotiating your contract

It is important that you consider certain matters when you are negotiating your contract for a new job. The following matters are particularly important:

(a) Will you have any job security? There are several important employment rights which you will not have until you have been continuously employed for two years (five years if your normal working week will be less than 16 hours). You should consider asking your prospective employer to agree to a contract term under which he will have to give you lengthy notice to terminate your contract. This is particularly the case if you are giving up an existing job where you already have rights in respect of unfair dismissal. You could also consider the possibility of negotiating a contract for a minimum fixed term, such as two or three years, but bear in mind that this kind of contract could restrict your own freedom.

(b) If you do enter into a contract for a fixed term, you should look carefully at the draft contract to see if your employer is seeking to exclude your rights relating to unfair dismissal and redundancy in the event of your contract not being renewed at the end of the fixed period. These exclusions could be effective, depending on the length of the contract.

Your Employment Rights

(c) It is also important to look hard at the draft contract to find out if your employer has the right to vary any of your contract terms without your agreement.
(d) If it is particularly important to you that your place of work or some other aspect of your work should not be varied in any way, it is desirable that this should be expressly stated.

Variation of your contract

Once a contract of employment has been entered into, neither you nor your employer can change the contract while it remains in force, unless there is some express provision for variation. If, for example, you are entitled to notice of at least three months to terminate your contract, your employer, to change the contract needs to give you notice of termination and offer you a new contract, on the new terms, at the end of the three months.

You will then have the choice of accepting the new contract or leaving, unless at that stage you have been continuously employed for at least two years (five years if you normally work less than 16 hours a week)

If you have that length of service and your employer is acting unreasonably in relation to the variation you can refuse to accept the new contract, leave the job and take your case to an Industrial Tribunal, claiming unfair dismissal (see Chapter 10).

Statement of terms

Most employees have the right to a written contract or a statement of the main terms of their employment. The statement should be supplied to you within 13 weeks after you start the employment. The most important matters to be covered in the statement are:

(a) The date when the employment began (and the date when it expires if this is a fixed term).
(b) The date of commencement of your period of continuous employment (this could include time with a previous employer if there has been a change in the ownership of the business).
(c) The scale or rate of remuneration or the method of calculating it.

Your Other Contract Rights

(d) The intervals at which you are to be paid (such as weekly or monthly).
(e) Any terms and conditions relating to hours of work.
(f) Terms relating to holidays and holiday pay.
(g) Terms relating to incapacity for work through sickness or injury and any provision for sick pay (these may be more favourable to you than the provisions for statutory sick pay which are explained in Chapter 6).
(h) Any terms and conditions relating to pension and pension schemes (or a statement that there is no pension scheme).
(i) The length of notice which your employer must give to terminate the contract (and the length of notice which you must give if you wish to terminate).
(j) Your job title.
(k) Any disciplinary rules (so long as there are 20 or more employees). These disciplinary rules are commonly contained in a separate document mentioned in the statement.
(l) Details of the grievance procedure, again if there are 20 or more employees. These details are also commonly referred to in a separate document.
(m) Whether there is a contracting-out certificate for pension purposes.

A statement of any variation in your contract should be supplied to you within one month after the variation.

You do not have the right to a statement of terms of employment if you ordinarily work outside Great Britain, if you work for fewer than 16 hours a week or if you are a civil servant or other Crown employee or work in the National Health Service or at the House of Commons. Certain seamen are also excluded.

If you do not receive a statement of terms to which you are entitled you can complain to an Industrial Tribunal. Complaints of this kind are usually brought when the employment has come to an end and it is a case of establishing your legal rights for the purpose of proceedings against your employer. The purpose of the complaint is not for the Tribunal to impose the terms which you ought to have agreed but to state the terms which you *have* agreed.

CHAPTER 4
Your Right to Time Off

The law gives you the right to time off (sometimes paid and sometimes not) for a number of specified purposes. Some of these rights are dealt with in later chapters, namely:

(a) Your right to time off for ante-natal treatment if you are pregnant (Chapter 5).
(b) Your right to time off for certain trade union activities (Chapter 13).
(c) Your right to time off to look for other work or for training if you have been given notice of dismissal on the ground of redundancy (Chapter 12).

There are two other rights which will be explained in this chapter.

Public duties

You have the right to unpaid leave for certain public duties, except in the following circumstances:

(a) If you are a part-time worker, working less than 16 hours per week.
(b) If you are in the police service.
(c) If you are a merchant seaman or share fisherman.
(d) If you ordinarily work outside Great Britain under your contract of employment.

The public duties for which you must be given leave include duties as a JP or a member of a local authority, statutory tribunal, health authority or Family Health Service Authority (or health board in Scotland), the governing body of an educational establishment maintained by a local education authority (or in Scotland a school or college council or a governing body of a central institution or a

Your Employment Rights

college of education) or a water authority (or river purification board in Scotland).

You must be allowed such time off as is reasonable in all the circumstances. The relevant circumstances include the effect on the business.

If you are not given the time off which should be allowed you can complain to an Industrial Tribunal which can award compensation.

Safety officers

You are entitled to paid leave for the purpose of performing your duties as a safety representative appointed by a recognised trade union. Your duties include investigating potential hazards and dangerous occurrences at the workplace and examining the causes of accidents, investigating complaints relating to health, safety or welfare at work; making representations to your employer about these matters; carrying out inspections; attending meetings of safety committees.

You are entitled to take off such time as is reasonable to enable you to perform the above functions. If your employer does not allow you the time off you can take the matter to an Industrial Tribunal within three months of the time when the employer failed to give you the time off or failed to pay you for time taken. The Tribunal can then award compensation.

CHAPTER 5
Your Rights if you are Pregnant

This is the one chapter in this book which is only for women. The law gives rights to pregnant women but it does not give rights to the husbands of pregnant women, such as paternity leave – at least not yet.

The rights which you have or may have as a pregnant employee are:

(a) The right not to be dismissed on account of your pregnancy.
(b) The right to return to work.
(c) The right to statutory maternity pay (SMP).
(d) The right to time off for ante-natal care.

Dismissal

Not all employees have the right not to be unfairly dismissed. The rules are explained in Chapter 10. One of the most important relates to length of service. You cannot complain of unfair dismissal if, at the effective date of termination of your employment, you have less than two years' continuous employment (five years if you work at least eight hours a week but fewer than 16 hours a week).

If you have the required length of service and meet the other conditions for claiming, you can bring an unfair dismissal claim if you are dismissed because you are pregnant. The dismissal will be automatically unfair. The same applies if you are selected for redundancy on account of your pregnancy.

There are, however, two exceptions. Your employer is entitled to dismiss you if your pregnancy prevents you from doing your work adequately (or will do so when the dismissal takes effect). He may also dismiss you if he would be in breach of some statutory duty by continuing to employ you in spite of your pregnancy.

Your Employment Rights

Even in these two cases, your employer must offer you an alternative post if there is a suitable vacancy. The terms and conditions of the new post must not be substantially less favourable to you than your existing contract terms.

What if you are dismissed before you have been continuously employed for two or five years (as the case may be)? Does this mean that you have no rights at all? There is a further important possibility. Even if you are dismissed after having been employed for only a short time, you could bring a claim of sex discrimination against your employer.

If you work in the public sector, for example as a civil servant or in local government, you may be able to bring a claim of sex discrimination under community law and win your claim automatically if you have been dismissed because you are pregnant. However, so far the Courts have adopted a different approach to cases involving private sector employees.

What the Courts do is look at the underlying reason for your dismissal. If you are dismissed while you are pregnant, it is unlikely to be the mere fact of your pregnancy that has caused your employer to dismiss you. It is more likely that it is some aspect of your pregnancy, such as the long absence from work which you may need, which has caused him to take this action. The question which the Courts will consider is whether a man requiring time off (for example, for an operation) would have been dismissed. If not, there has been sex discrimination against you.

Another reason sometimes given by employers, especially if the job involves reception work or work in a shop or showroom, is that the public would find you unattractive because of your advanced state of pregnancy. The Tribunal would then consider whether a male employee would be sacked by that particular employer because he was obese or ugly. If not, the Tribunal is likely to find in your favour.

Sometimes employers give a false reason for dismissing pregnant employees. For example, your employer may pretend that you are redundant or that your work is poor. If your employer gives a reason which is shown to be false, the Industrial Tribunal may be ready to treat this dishonesty as giving rise to an inference of sex discrimination.

Your Rights if you are Pregnant

Your right to return to work

There are a few employees who do not have the right to return to work after their pregnancy or confinement. You do not have this right if:

(a) You ordinarily work outside Great Britain.
(b) You are normally employed for fewer than 16 hours per week (but you may have the right if you work at least 8 hours and have five years' service).
(c) You are employed in the police service or you are a share fisherman.

In order to establish whether you will have a right to return to work after your confinement, some fairly complicated arithmetic may be required. The starting point is to find out the week when the baby is expected. This week is known as the expected week of confinement (EWC). You must then count back for eleven weeks and go back to the beginning of the eleventh week. This date is known as the qualifying date. You will have the right to return to work if, on the qualifying date, you have been continuously employed by your employer for at least two years and if your absence from work is wholly or partly because of your pregnancy or confinement.

There are some strict conditions to be complied with to exercise your right to return to work. These conditions are as follows:

(a) You must continue to be employed until the qualifying date as mentioned above, ie the beginning of the eleventh week before the EWC (unless you are dismissed earlier because your pregnancy makes you incapable of doing your work or would cause your employer to break some statutory requirement if he continued to employ you).
(b) You must inform your employer in writing at least 21 days before your absence begins that you will be absent from work wholly or partly because of pregnancy or confinement and that you intend to return to work with your employer. The notice must also state the EWC or (if your confinement has already occurred) the date of the confinement. If it is not reasonably practicable for you to give the notice at least 21 days before your absence begins, you must give the notice as soon as it is reasonably practicable.

Your Employment Rights

(c) If requested by your employer you must produce a medical certificate stating the EWC.
(d) During the seven weeks starting with the beginning of the EWC (or date of confinement) which you have notified to your employer, you may be requested by your employer to give written confirmation that you still intend to return to work. You must give this confirmation within 14 days of receiving the request for it. If that is not reasonably practicable you must give the confirmation as soon as it is reasonably practicable.
(e) There is a date by which you must return to work in order to preserve your right to return. It is necessary to work out what is the 29-week period in which week 1 is the week in which your actual confinement falls. You must return to work before the end of this 29-week period.
(f) You must then give written notice to your employer at least 21 days before you return to work. The notice must state the date on which you propose to return (the notified day of return). It is, of course, essential to give the notice before the end of week 26 in the 29-week period mentioned above.

You may then postpone your return for up to four weeks beyond the 29-week period if you are unfit for work on the notified day of return. However, before the notified day of return you must give your employer a medical certificate.

The following is an example of a straightforward case:

(a) Your baby is expected on Wednesday 17 November 1993. The week commencing 14 November is therefore the EWC.
(b) You must count back from 14 November for 11 weeks, to 29 August 1993. You must not give up work until that week.
(c) You will also need to have been continuously employed for at least two years on 29 August 1993.
(d) You decide to leave work at the end of that week, on 3 September. You must give your employer notice in writing at least 21 days earlier. To be on the safe side, do not let the 21 days nearly run out. Give the notice to your employer on, say, 2 August. Remember to state in the notice that you will be absent from work because of your pregnancy and that you intend to return to work. Remember also to state that the EWC is the week commencing 14 November.

Your Rights if you are Pregnant

(e) You go into hospital and have your baby a week early, on 10 November.

(f) On 29 November you receive a letter from your employer asking you to give written confirmation that you still intend to return to work. You must write back that week or the following week, ie within 14 days, confirming that you do intend to return.

(g) You must then count forward for 29 weeks from 10 November, the date of your confinement, in order to find out when you must return to work. Week 1 is the week commencing 7 November, the week in which your confinement fell. Week 29 will be the week commencing 22 May 1994. You must return to work before the end of that week.

(h) You decide to go back to work on 23 May. You must give written notice to your employer at least 21 days earlier, stating that you intend to return to work on 23 May. To be on the safe side, give the notice before the end of April.

There is one further important exception to your right to return to work. This exception only applies if, immediately before your absence from work, the number of employees employed by your employer (and also any associated company) did not exceed five. In these circumstances, your employer can refuse to allow you to return if it is not reasonably practicable for him to take you back and if there is no suitable alternative employment.

Any employer, not only a small firm as mentioned above, can refuse to give you your old job back, if it is not reasonably practicable to take you back in that job, but only if suitable alternative employment is offered to you.

If you are not allowed to return to work in accordance with your statutory rights, you can take your case to an Industrial Tribunal in order to claim compensation for unfair dismissal and, if appropriate, a redundancy payment. You must submit your Tribunal application within three months after the notified day of return.

Statutory maternity pay

Most employees have the right to statutory maternity pay (SMP). The only kind of job which is excluded is service in the armed forces (including the reserve forces) and also certain jobs as a foreign-going mariner.

Your Employment Rights

There are, however, a number of conditions. The most important are as follows:

(a) It is necessary first of all to work back 15 weeks from the date before your baby is due. This week is known as the qualifying week (QW). You do not have the right to SMP unless you have been continuously employed by your employer for at least 26 weeks up to and including the QW.
(b) You must have normal weekly earnings not less than the lower earnings limit for National Insurance purposes. The current figure is £46.
(c) You must still be pregnant at the 11th week before your expected week of confinement or have already been confined by that time.
(d) You must give notice to your employer of the date when you intend to stop work because of your pregnancy. This notice must be given at least 21 days before your absence is due to begin. If this is not reasonably practicable the notice must be given as soon as it is reasonably practicable.
(e) You must provide your employer with medical evidence of your pregnancy.

The SMP is paid to you for a maximum period of 18 weeks. The period for which the SMP is paid is referred to as the maternity pay period. This period cannot start more than 11 weeks before the EWC. It must include the six weeks before the EWC, the EWC itself and the six weeks after the EWC.

The maternity pay period will come to an end, and you will lose your right to maternity pay, once you go back to work, whether for your old employer or for another employer. You will also lose the right if you are taken into legal custody or go outside the European Community.

There are two rates of SMP. The lower rate is currently £46.30 and the higher rate is 90 per cent of your normal weekly earnings. In order to work out whether you qualify for the higher rate, it is necessary to work back again from the EWC. You must work back for 15 weeks from the EWC in order to arrive at the qualifying week. If you have two years' continuous employment up to and including the qualifying week, you will be entitled to the higher rate for the first six weeks of the maternity pay period and the lower rate for the remaining 12 weeks. If you normally work eight hours or more a week but less than 16 hours, you will need to

Your Rights if you are Pregnant

have five years' continuous employment up to and including the qualifying week. If you do not have the necessary length of service, you will receive the lower rate of SMP for the whole of the maternity pay period.

If you do not receive the SMP to which you are entitled, you *cannot* take your case to an Industrial Tribunal. You should apply to the DSS and ask for a formal decision from an Adjudication Officer. If the decision is in your favour and your employer still does not pay, he can be prosecuted.

Time off for ante-natal care

You have the right to time off for ante-natal care unless you ordinarily work outside Great Britain under your contract of employment or unless you are employed in the police service. There are also exceptions, rarely likely to occur in practice, for share fishermen and merchant seamen.

You are entitled to *paid* time off during working hours for ante-natal care, except where your employer has reasonable grounds for refusing. For each appointment except the first you must, if your employer asks you to do so, produce a certificate from your doctor, midwife or health visitor and an appointment card.

If you are not allowed the time off you can submit an Industrial Tribunal application within three months after your employer's refusal.

CHAPTER 6
Your Rights if you are Sick

Not all employees have the right to keep their jobs if they are off sick. If you do not have the right to complain of unfair dismissal (the conditions are explained in Chapter 10) your employer can dismiss you, so long as he acts within the terms of the contract; for example, by giving you the required notice. This means that until you have two years' continuous service (five years' if you work at least eight but less than 16 hours a week) you will be at risk of being dismissed if you take time off.

Once you have the right not to be unfairly dismissed, your employer must act reasonably before dismissing you. He should assess the situation properly, seek to obtain a medical report and discuss the whole matter with you. In particular, it would almost certainly be an unfair dismissal if you have had a single absence from work and if your employer dismisses you during that absence without giving careful consideration to the prospects of your return to work and discussing the prospects with you.

Your contract of employment or statement of terms should tell you what pay you will be entitled to while you are off work. Many contracts give employees more favourable rights than the right to statutory sick pay mentioned below. For example, your contract may state that you will be paid in full for the first 13 weeks of your absence and that you will be entitled to half pay for the next 13 weeks.

Statutory sick pay

Your right to statutory sick pay (SSP) will arise if you have four or more consecutive days of incapacity for work. These four days can include a non-working day, such as a Sunday. The SSP is payable for every day off work after the first three days, up to a maximum of 28 weeks.

Your Employment Rights

Your employer is entitled to notification of your continuing absence and the reason for it up to once a week. He is also entitled to evidence of your continuing incapacity, but this can be self-certification for the first seven days.

The rate of SSP depends on your weekly rate of pay. The details are as follows:

(a) If your weekly wage is less than £54 you will not be entitled to SSP at all.
(b) If your wage is between £54 and £190, then the rate of SSP is £45.30.
(c) If your weekly wage is more than £190, the rate of SSP is £52.50.

The above figures are increased at regular intervals and the figures given above are those in force at 6 April 1992.

If you are off work four times for at least four days each time in any 12-month period, your employer can tell the Department of Social Security (DSS) who can ask you to visit your doctor next time you are off sick, so that your doctor can submit a report. Then if you are off again your employer, if he has doubts about the reason for your absence, can suspend your SSP and notify the DSS who will investigate the matter.

You will not be entitled to SSP in the following circumstances:

(a) If you are over state pension age.
(b) If you are employed for a fixed period of no more than three months.
(c) If you have claimed state benefits or SSP from a previous employment within eight weeks before the start of your incapacity.
(d) If you are pregnant and off work during the 18-week period starting 11 weeks before the expected week of confinement.
(e) If you are outside the EC on the first day of your absence from work.
(f) If you are in legal custody on that day.
(g) If you are a member of the armed forces or the reserve forces.

If you do not receive the SSP which you have claimed, you can refer the matter to an Adjudication Officer at the DSS. If the decision is in your favour and the money still not paid, you can claim the money by taking proceedings in the County Court.

CHAPTER 7
Your Right to Safety at Work

If you are injured at work you will not automatically be entitled to compensation. The accident may be entirely your own fault; it may be a freak accident which is nobody's fault; it may be caused by some outsider who has nothing to do with your employer and who cannot be traced.

There are, however, many kinds of accident which do give you a right to claim compensation from your employer. The following are examples:

(a) You are injured because the premises where you work are unsafe and your employer should have known that repairs were required.
(b) The accident is caused by a fault in the machinery or equipment at work. Your employer should have known about this fault or it would have been avoided by regular maintenance.
(c) A vehicle which you are driving or travelling in as part of your employment crashes because of a mechanical fault. The vehicle has not been properly serviced.
(d) You are not provided with necessary safety equipment, such as gloves or goggles.
(e) Dangerous machinery is not fenced.
(f) Your employer requires or allows your work to be done in an unnecessarily dangerous way.
(g) Your employer disregards the requirements of an Act of Parliament which has been passed to ensure your safety.
(h) You are injured because one of your fellow employees is careless in the way in which he does his work.

The last example highlights one of the important rules which can entitle you to bring a claim. Your employer is held responsible for the carelessness of your fellow employees, so long as they are doing something within the course of their employment.

Your Employment Rights

Your employer is also responsible for his own negligence (ie carelessness), breach of any statutory duty which is imposed on him and for his failure to provide a safe system of working.

If your accident at work is caused or contributed to by your own negligence, any compensation awarded to you could be reduced on that account. The law, however, generally demands a higher standard from the employer who makes the rules than from individual employees.

If you have an accident at work and wish to claim compensation, you should submit a claim which your employer will then generally pass on to his insurance company. If the claim is not met you are entitled to take legal proceedings in the Courts and claim damages, which will include damages for pain and suffering as well as any financial losses.

There is a time limit of three years for bringing proceedings, but this time limit can be extended in certain circumstances (where, for example, a medical condition is caused by your working conditions but does not show itself within the three-year period).

Medical suspension pay

If your work involves, eg, exposure to radiation and your employer suspends you following a regular medical check, you could have the right to be paid your contract wage for up to 26 weeks. You must, however, have been employed for at least one month when the suspension begins and your Industrial Tribunal claim must be lodged within three months from that date.

If you are dismissed in these circumstances you may have the right to complain of unfair dismissal, even though you have less than two years' continuous service.

The main exclusions are overseas employment, police service, share fishermen and part-time employees with less than five years' service.

CHAPTER 8
Your Right to Equal Pay

Your right to equal pay is a right to the same rate of pay as an employee of the opposite sex, known as the 'comparator'. Most claims are made by women, but you can also claim if you are a man and the comparator is a woman.

The claim need not be about pay or only about pay. If your comparator has a contract which is better than yours in some other respect, then you can claim the improved contract terms. Claims can be about anything which is covered by your contract or the comparator's contract, including paid meal breaks, sickness pay, health insurance, luncheon vouchers and other fringe benefits.

The first condition, to bring an equal pay claim, is that both you and your comparator must be employed at an establishment in Great Britain. It may also be sufficient, however, if you work on British ships or aircraft or on an oil platform in British waters.

Subject to this condition, all employees have the right to claim equal pay if a suitable comparator or comparators can be identified. There is no qualifying period for which you must be employed before a claim can be brought. You can claim equal pay even if you have been employed for only one day. There are, however, special provisions for members of the armed forces. Certain agricultural workers are covered by a special statutory order.

To bring a claim, you must be 'in the same employment' as the comparator. This does not mean that you have to work for the same employer. It is enough if you work for two associated companies. As long as you are employed by the same employer or associated companies, it is not even necessary for you to work at the same establishment. You can work at different establishments, as long as employees generally at the two establishments are covered by the same collective agreement or have contract terms and conditions which do not vary greatly as between the two establishments.

You can specify more than one comparator of the opposite sex. If you are to succeed in your claim, the first step is for you to prove one of three things:

(a) That your job and your comparator's job have been given the same rating under a job evaluation scheme; or
(b) That you and your comparator are employed on 'like work'; or
(c) That you and your comparator are employed on work of equal value.

Most claims are 'like work' or 'equal value' claims. In a *like work* claim, the two jobs must be the same or broadly similar. There can be differences between them, as long as these differences are of no practical importance, so that they would normally be ignored in fixing pay rates or other contract terms. You can bring an *equal value* claim even if the two jobs are totally different. The question to be considered will be whether the two jobs are of equal value, having regard to the demands of each of them.

The comparison of the jobs in an equal value claim has to be referred by the Industrial Tribunal to an independent expert. He or she measures the demands of the jobs under a number of different headings and awards points to each job under each heading. For example, what are the physical demands of each job? How much concentration or other mental effort is required? Are any special skills demanded? Does the job involve unpleasant working conditions? How much responsibility does the job involve? If the total number of points given to your job is at least as great as the number given to the comparator's job, then your job will be of equal value to the comparator's.

The need to involve an expert means that equal value claims take much longer and (if you are legally represented) can be much more expensive than other equal pay cases, such as like work claims.

Defences to equal pay claims

Your claim can be defeated if your employer shows that your job and your comparator's job have been given different ratings under a job evaluation scheme. The scheme must, however, be carried out properly and objectively and it must not be tainted by sex discrimination. This defence applies to equal value and like work claims.

There is a further important defence to any equal pay claim, whether based on like work, equal value or job evaluation. Your employer can point to some 'material factor' which explains the difference in pay. It could be, for example, that your comparator is better qualified or more experienced than you. As long as the material factor is unrelated to the difference in sex, your claim could be defeated.

In equal value cases, any material factor defence is commonly considered before the Industrial Tribunal refers the job comparison to an independent expert.

The meaning of 'pay'

When you are comparing your rate of pay with that of your comparator, it is important to compare like with like. The relevant comparison is generally between the hourly rates of pay rather than the amounts in the pay packet each week. If your comparator takes home more than you do each week, it could be for any of the following reasons:

(a) He works longer hours.
(b) He works more overtime.
(c) You work on the day shift but he works on the night shift and receives a shift premium.

There could nevertheless be an equal pay claim in (b) above, if your comparator's contract gives him a guaranteed amount of overtime each week and if you would like to have a similar term in your contract.

European law

Our own law on equal pay has been greatly influenced by European Community law.

There are also cases where you may be able to bring a claim because gaps in our own law have been filled by Community law. For example, if you are paid less than the person who did your job immediately before you and that person is of the opposite sex, then you may have a claim under Community law, even though our own Equal Pay Act does not cover claims of this kind. The

Your Employment Rights

employer can of course still try to defeat your claim by showing that there is some material factor, apart from the difference in sex, which explains the difference in pay.

Compensation and other remedies

If you succeed in an equal pay claim, there are two ways in which you can benefit:

(a) The Industrial Tribunal will make an order declaring your rights. The effect is that in future you will be entitled to the same rate of pay and contract terms as your comparator.
(b) The Tribunal can also award back pay. There is no limit on the amount which can be awarded, but in calculating the amount the Tribunal cannot have regard to any period which was more than two years before the date when you lodged your Tribunal application.

CHAPTER 9
Your Right to Equal Opportunity

You have a right to do your job without any sex discrimination against you. Your employer must not treat you worse than he would treat someone else:

- because you are a man; or
- because you are a woman; or
- because you are married.

Consider a few examples. In all these cases your employer is breaking the law.

1. You are a woman. You have worked for many years in a factory. You apply for promotion to supervisor. Your boss says no, because he reckons that the men on the shop floor would not take kindly to having a woman as a supervisor.
2. You are a man. You are suspended without pay for swearing at your boss. A woman who works alongside you is always doing the same thing and is always being let off because she is a woman.
3. You are a married woman. You apply to go on a training course. Instead, the company send a young woman who is unmarried. They are not prepared to waste money on training you because of your family commitments.

In a few cases employers are allowed to discriminate. The main example is maternity pay and maternity leave. Many pregnant woman have these rights, which are explained in Chapter 5. If you are a man whose wife is pregnant, you cannot insist on paternity pay or paternity leave – yet!

Racial discrimination

You also have the right to do your job without any racial

Your Employment Rights

discrimination against you. Your employer must not treat you worse than he would treat someone else:

- because of your colour; or
- because of the ethnic group you belong to; or
- because of where you come from; or
- because of your nationality.

In the following cases your employer is breaking the law:

1. You are black. You work as a shop assistant with a manager and two other assistants. The manager leaves. The owner promotes one of the other assistants, not you, even though you have been there longer and do the work better, because this other assistant is white.
2. Your family originally came from India. Because of your colour, you are not allowed to sit with the white workers in the works canteen.
3. You are Jewish. You work in a company's export department. You are transferred to a worse job in another department. The reason is that the company has won a big order from an Arab customer. It is felt that this customer may object to dealing with you because you are Jewish.

Sexual harassment

You have the right to do your job without having to face any sexual harassment. The law forbids sexual harassment at work, just like any other kind of sex discrimination. The following are examples of sexual harassment. In each case what is being done to you is against the law:

1. You are the only woman working on the shop floor. One of the men is always making suggestive remarks to you. You are upset by this but the foreman does nothing about it, despite your complaints.
2. You are a woman. Your boss is a man. He keeps asking you to go away with him for the weekend. He tells you that you have no future with the company unless you agree. All this gets on your nerves. You dread coming into work.
3. You are a young man. Your boss is a homosexual. He makes

Your Right to Equal Opportunity

physical advances to you one day when you are alone with him in the office.

Racial harassment

Racial harassment is also forbidden, just like any other kind of racial discrimination. In the following cases, what happens to you is against the law:

1. You are a black worker in a factory. Some of the white workers are always making racist remarks to try to upset you. They succeed. You get very upset. The foreman knows what is happening and takes no action.
2. You are black. You work in a typing pool. The other women are all white. You are as good a typist as they are. One of the partners of the firm never complains about their mistakes but is always picking on you. He shouts at you and rants and rages whenever there is the smallest mistake. He does this because you are black.

If you are distressed by racial or sexual harassment at work you can claim compensation. You should claim against your employer. You should also claim against the person or persons who are actually guilty of the harassment.

Sometimes sexual or racial harassment is so bad that the victim is driven out of his or her job. You can also claim compensation, however, if you have stayed in the job. You have the right to be allowed to get on with your job and not to be treated as a sex object or as a freak because of your sex or your colour.

Remember that in very bad cases racial or sexual harassment can be a crime. If you are beaten up or even thumped once because of your colour, this is a criminal assault. If a man attacks you and puts his hands on your breasts this is an indecent assault. You should go to the police.

Indirect discrimination

The law also forbids indirect racial and sex discrimination. What does this mean? The following is a 'translation' of the complicated definition to be found in the legislation:

Your Employment Rights

(a) life is made difficult for you at work, or you miss out on some benefit;
(b) this is because of some rule or decision by your employer;
(c) this rule or decision tends to work against people of your sex or racial group (or you and other married people); and
(d) your employer cannot justify the rule of decision.

Take an example:

> You are a Sikh, working as a car sales rep. You are told that the management has decided that all the sales reps must in future be clean shaven, because this would look better. Your are told that you will have to shave off your beard if you want to keep your job. As a Sikh, you cannot shave off your beard. There has been indirect racial discrimination against you.

What can you do about discrimination?

Suppose there has been racial or sex discrimination against you. What can you do about it? You can take your case to an Industrial Tribunal and the way to go about this is explained in Chapter 15. There is one important point to remember. You must lodge your claim *within three months*. This time limit is very strict and rarely extended.

If you take your case to a Tribunal and win, what will you get out of it? The Tribunal will tell your employer that he has done wrong. Occasionally the employer is told how he should put matters right. But the main thing which the Tribunal can do for you is order your employer to pay you money, to help compensate you for what has happened. Even if the discrimination against you has not cost you any money, you can be awarded compensation for injured feelings.

You may not be awarded any money if the discrimination which you are complaining about was indirect. Compensation is not payable for indirect discrimination if it was unintentional.

Victimisation

You may be worried about taking your employer to a Tribunal to complain of discrimination. It could damage your chances of promotion. It could even lead to the sack. The law does give you some protection as long as your claim is genuine. Whether you

Your Right to Equal Opportunity

win or lose, you will be able to make a further claim for compensation if you are treated badly at work because:

- you have complained to your employer about discrimination; or
- you have taken your case to a Tribunal; or
- you have threatened to go to a Tribunal; or
- you have given evidence in someone else's discrimination case.

There is a strict time limit for victimisation claims as well. Your complaint must be lodged *within three months* of the victimisation taking place.

Help with your case

Discrimination cases are difficult. Is there anywhere you can go for help? There is some advice in Chapter 15 on places where you can go for help with any kind of employment claim. There are also specialist bodies to advise you if you want to complain about discrimination: the Equal Opportunities Commission or the Commission for Racial Equality (details of both are given in Chapter 15).

Other chapters

You will find that there are several other chapters in this book in which the possibility of a racial or sex discrimination claim is mentioned. Chapter 1 deals with claims by you as a job applicant; Chapter 5 deals with your rights when pregnant; Chapters 10, 11 and 12 deal with your rights if you lose your job; Chapter 14 deals with your pension rights and other rights as an ex-employee.

CHAPTER 10
Your Rights if you are Sacked

If you are dismissed from your job, you will be entitled to bring a claim against your employer, or former employer, if:

(a) you have been wrongfully dismissed; or
(b) you have been unfairly dismissed; or
(c) your dismissal involves racial or sex discrimination or victimisation.

The distinction between wrongful dismissal and unfair dismissal is not commonly understood. A *wrongful* dismissal is one which involves a breach of contract by your employer. Your remedy is to bring Court proceedings. In principle, a claim against your employer for breach of contract is dealt with in the same way as any other claim for breach of contract, such as a claim for repayment of a debt or a claim against a builder who has failed to do agreed work to your house.

Unfair dismissal, on the other hand, does not necessarily involve any breach of contract by the employer. He may have acted strictly in accordance with the contract but nevertheless infringed your rights by dismissing you unfairly. Your dismissal will be unfair if it is not for a sufficient reason or if your employer has acted unreasonably in deciding to dismiss you or in the way the dismissal is carried out.

There are three important practical differences between claims for wrongful dismissal and those for unfair dismissal:

(a) If you have been wrongfully dismissed, you should bring proceedings in the Courts; if you have been unfairly dismissed, you should complain to an Industrial Tribunal.
(b) The time limit for complaining of wrongful dismissal is six years, although most actions are started very much earlier; the time limit for complaining of unfair dismissal is only three months.

Your Employment Rights

(c) You can apply for legal aid in order to take proceedings for wrongful dismissal; there is no legal aid for claims of unfair dismissal (or any other Industrial Tribunal claims).

In all three of the above respects, complaints about racial or sex discrimination are dealt with in the same way as complaints about unfair dismissal.

Your various rights can overlap. For example, your dismissal may be both wrongful and unfair and it may be necessary to bring Court proceedings as well as Industrial Tribunal proceedings. If your dismissal involves racial or sex discrimination, you might be able to complain about unfair dismissal as well as about the discrimination.

Each of your dismissal rights will now be explained in turn.

Wrongful dismissal

The following are ways in which your employer could be breaking his contract with you by dismissing you:

(a) You have a contract for a fixed period and your employer dismisses you while there is still time to run on the contract.
(b) Your employer fails to give you the minimum length of notice required under the terms of your contract.
(c) Your employer fails to follow the procedure laid down in your contract; for example, by dismissing you for misconduct without a disciplinary hearing, even though your contract entitles you to a hearing.

The most common complaint of wrongful dismissal is the second kind mentioned above – failure to give the notice required under the terms of the contract. It is not always an easy matter, however, to establish how much notice you are entitled to. It is necessary to look not only at the terms expressly stated in your contract but also at further terms written in by statute and other terms which could be implied by the Courts.

Whatever your contract of employment says, and even if your employer has never given you a contract or a statement of contract terms, you will be entitled to a minimum period of notice so long as all the following conditions apply:

(a) You have been continuously employed for at least one month, with a normal working week of 16 hours or more, or for at

Your Rights if you are Sacked

least five years, with a normal working week of eight hours or more.
(b) You are not a servant of the Crown, such as a member of the civil service or the armed forces.
(c) You work in Great Britain. Alternatively, if you are currently working outside Great Britain, you ordinarily work in Great Britain for the same employer.
(d) You were not taken on for a specific task which was expected to last for no more than three months; or you were taken on to do such a task, but you have in fact been continuously employed for more than three months.
(e) You are not employed as master or seaman on a sea-going British ship with a gross registered tonnage of 80 tons or more or as skipper or seaman on a registered fishing boat.

If you meet all the above conditions, you will have a statutory right to minimum notice. The notice which you will be entitled to is as follows:

(a) One week's notice if you have been continuously employed for less than two years.
(b) Two weeks' notice once you have been continuously employed for two years.
(c) One week's notice for each further year of continuous employment until you have been continuously employed for 12 years.
(d) 12 weeks' notice if you have been employed for 12 years or more.

All these references to continuous employment mean employment by the same employer, with one important exception. If the business in which you work is transferred as a going concern, you become the employee of the new owner of the business and continuity of employment is maintained. You should also note that you may be regarded as having been continuously employed even if there are breaks in your employment; for example, because you have been off sick or on maternity leave.

The starting point, if you have been given notice, is to count your years of employment and work out the statutory minimum notice to which you are entitled – unless, of course, you are a Crown employee or belong to one of the other groups who do not have the statutory rights to minimum notice.

Your Employment Rights

This is not the end of the matter, however. You should then look at your contract or statement of terms of employment. If this document specifies a minimum notice which is longer than the statutory minimum you are entitled to this longer notice.

You may be entitled to more than the statutory minimum notice, even if you do not have the benefit of any express contract terms giving you longer notice. In certain cases, particularly where you are a full-time director or manager or occupy some other senior post, the Courts will be prepared to imply a contract term giving you the right to reasonable notice. This notice could be considerably longer than the statutory minimum. If you are a senior employee, even if you have been employed for only a short time, you may be entitled to receive six or even 12 months' notice.

If you have an express or implied contract term regarding notice, your employer must, of course, give you the required notice under your contract even if you do not qualify for the statutory minimum notice.

Justified dismissals

There are circumstances in which your employer may lawfully dismiss you without giving you the notice which would normally be required and indeed without giving you any notice at all. If you break your contract with your employer by committing some act of gross misconduct, such as stealing from your employer, you cannot expect to be able to hold your employer to his contract with you.

Your rights if you are wrongfully dismissed

You may be able to argue that you are still ready to carry out your part of the contract and that your employer must continue to pay you until proper steps have been taken to dismiss you, in accordance with your contract.

In practice, however, most employees who are wrongfully dismissed accept the position and bring proceedings in the County Court (or the High Court if the claim is a big one) to claim damages.

In order to work out the damages which you can claim, the starting point is the extra money which your employer would have had to pay you if you had been given the notice to which you were entitled or if your fixed-term contract had been allowed to run its full course. You can also claim the value of any fringe

Your Rights if you are Sacked

benefits for the relevant period. The following amounts will be deducted in order to arrive at the figure for the damages:

(a) The tax and National Insurance payments which would have been deducted from your pay.
(b) Any money which you have earned during the period or which you would have been able to earn if you had made reasonable efforts to find a new job.
(c) Any unemployment benefit or other State benefit which you have received.

You will not be entitled to any additional money to compensate you for injured feelings.

Unfair dismissal

Parliament has given certain employees the right not to be unfairly dismissed. Many employees, however, do not have this right. Some have not yet acquired it; some have lost it; some will never have it.

It is possible that you will not have the right because of the kind of work you do. However, there are not many jobs of this kind. The following are the main examples:

(a) Jobs where you are based outside Great Britain (although you may have the right if you work on a British ship).
(b) Posts in the police and prison services.
(c) Service in the armed forces.
(d) Certain other Crown posts (but most civil servants do have the right).
(e) Work as a share fisherman.

The above exceptions affect only a small minority of the working population in Great Britain. However, there is one far more serious exclusion. You do not acquire the right not to be unfairly dismissed until you have been continuously employed for at least two years, with a normal working week of 16 hours or more. If your normal working week is eight hours or more but less than 16, you will need to be continuously employed for five years (there are special rules where the hours have changed). A change in the ownership of the business will not normally affect the continuity of your employment; nor will certain breaks in the employment.

Your Employment Rights

This means that when you start work, or change jobs, your employer can dismiss you with impunity for the first two years (or five years if you normally work between eight and 16 hours a week). It does not matter how unreasonable the dismissal is. You have no rights in the matter, so long as the employer complies with the terms of your contract and so long as your dismissal:

(a) does not involve racial or sex discrimination;
(b) is not on the ground of your trade union membership or activities;
(c) is not on the ground of your non-membership of a union.

This reinforces the advice already given in Chapter 2. When you are starting a new job, particularly if you are giving up a job in which you have been employed for a long time, you should try to negotiate a contract under which you will be employed for a minimum specified period or be entitled to a substantial period of notice. Otherwise you could find yourself out on the street with no right of action at all.

Your right to complain of unfair dismissal can also be lost or excluded in the following circumstances:

(a) If you continue working after the normal retiring age for employees who work for your employer and hold similar positions to your own (or the age of 65 if there is no normal retiring age).
(b) If you have a contract for a fixed term of one year or more and your employer unfairly refuses to renew your contract, so long as the contract contains a provision expressly excluding your right to complain of unfair dismissal.
(c) If you are dismissed while taking part in official industrial action (or during a lock-out), so long as your employer does not act selectively in dismissing you or taking back other employees within the following three months.
(d) If you are dismissed while taking part in unofficial industrial action (whether selectively or not).
(e) If a Minister of the Crown has certified that you have been dismissed for the purpose of safeguarding national security. This could happen, for example, if you work for a company which is about to receive a sensitive defence contract and the Secretary of State for Defence considers that you are a security risk because of your political activities.

Your Rights if you are Sacked

The way in which (c) and (d) work in practice is explained in more detail in Chapter 13.

The reason for the dismissal
If you have the right to complain of unfair dismissal, you will also have the right to ask your employer for a statement of the reasons for your dismissal. You may also have this right to ask for reasons even if you do not have the right to complain of unfair dismissal; for example, because you are above normal retiring age or because you have been dismissed while taking part in industrial action.

If you complain of unfair dismissal, the first question for the Industrial Tribunal is to establish the reason or main reason for the dismissal. If your employer has given a statement of reasons, the employer's reasons will not necessarily be accepted by the Tribunal. Once the reason for dismissal has been established by the Tribunal, there are three possibilities. The first possibility is that the reason for your dismissal makes the dismissal automatically unfair because:

(a) You have been dismissed because you are pregnant and your case does not fall within one of the exceptions explained in Chapter 5.
(b) You have been dismissed for membership (or proposed membership) or taking part in the activities of an independent trade union.
(c) You have been dismissed because you are not a member of a union (or some particular union) and are not willing to join.

Your rights if you are dismissed for one of the reasons mentioned in (b) and (c) are explained in more detail in Chapter 13. You have these rights even if you have been employed for less than two years when you are dismissed.

The second possibility is that you have been dismissed for a reason which the Tribunal does not regard as being a substantial and justifiable reason. An obvious example would be if you were dismissed on racial grounds or because of your sex. If the reason for dismissing you is not one which could justify your dismissal, your claim will succeed.

The third possibility is that you have been dismissed for a reason which is capable of making your dismissal a fair one. These reasons are:

Your Employment Rights

(a) A reason related to your capability or qualifications.
(b) A reason related to your conduct.
(c) Redundancy.
(d) Some statutory duty or restriction which would make it unlawful for you to continue to do your work or for your employer to let you do so.
(e) Some other substantial reason which would justify your dismissal.

In (a), the word 'capability' covers both fitness and competence. Dismissal because of a long-term absence through illness and dismissal because the job is beyond you would both be covered by 'capability'.

An example of a reason related to your qualifications would be dismissal from a driving job because you have been disqualified from driving.

An example of (d) would be if you are a foreign national and you need a work permit which has expired.

Most dismissals are for one of the reasons given in (a), (b) or (c). The first two of these are considered below. Dismissals for redundancy are dealt with in Chapter 12. We shall see in that chapter that your dismissal on the ground of redundancy may also be an unfair dismissal.

If the Tribunal finds that you have been dismissed for one of the reasons mentioned above, that is not the end of the matter. Your claim will succeed if the Industrial Tribunal decides that your employer acted unreasonably, in the circumstances, in deciding to dismiss you or in the way in which the dismissal was handled.

Examples of unfair dismissals

The following are examples of cases where your claim for unfair dismissal could succeed because your employer has acted unreasonably:

(a) You have been dismissed for unsatisfactory job performance or minor disciplinary offences without having been given adequate warnings and a fair chance to improve.
(b) You have been dismissed because you have been off work for several months and your employer has not made reasonable efforts to find out when you will be fit to return to work, by discussing the matter with you and asking you to attend for a medical examination.

Your Rights if you are Sacked

(c) You have been dismissed for misconduct and your employer has not given you a fair hearing and a chance to answer the allegations against you.

(d) The decision to dismiss you is not consistent with the decisions in other cases. For example, you have been dismissed for fighting, but another employee, whose record is no better than yours, has only been warned for a similar offence.

If you are dismissed for serious misconduct, your dismissal may be held to be fair even though it is a first offence and you have never received any warnings. Examples could include dismissal for stealing from your employer or fellow employees, selling or giving away confidential information or assaulting a fellow employee.

You may also be held to have been fairly dismissed even though you have in fact received a raw deal. For example:

> You are accused of stealing. Your employers investigate fully and fairly and decide that you are guilty of the offence. This was a reasonable decision on the information available. Later on you are prosecuted and completely cleared. In spite of your innocence, the dismissal was fair, because your employers acted reasonably on the information available to them at the time.

Compensation and other remedies

If you are successful in your unfair dismissal claim, the Industrial Tribunal must consider ordering the employer to give you your job back or give you another job, if you wish to go back. In practice, however, reinstatement (or re-engagement in some other post) is rarely ordered. In many cases the employee does not wish to go back and in others it is not practicable for the employer to take the employee back.

There is, however, one important special case. If you believe that you have been dismissed for trade union membership or activities or non-membership of a trade union, you can apply to an Industrial Tribunal for interim relief. The purpose of this application is to maintain the status quo. The procedure, and the strict time limit, are explained in Chapter 15.

In most cases, if you win your case, the Tribunal will simply order your employer to pay compensation. The standard elements of any compensation award are:

(a) The basic award.

Your Employment Rights

(b) The compensatory award.
(c) A sum for loss of statutory rights.

The *basic award* is equal to the redundancy pay which you would have been entitled to if you had been made redundant. The rules for calculating this amount are set out in Chapter 12.

The next standard award is the *compensatory award*. The purpose of this award, as the name implies, is to compensate you for the net pay (after tax and National Insurance) which you have lost or are likely to lose as a result of your dismissal. It is not possible to lay down any hard and fast rules about the calculation of the compensatory award. The Tribunal is obliged only to award whatever sum is 'just and equitable' in the circumstances. Different Tribunals may take different views.

The matter is usually approached in two stages. First of all the Tribunal decides on a sum to compensate you for the earnings which you have already lost, up to the date of the hearing. Then, if you are still out of work (or employed at a lower rate of pay than in your old job), the Tribunal decides what would be a reasonable period, such as six months or 12 months, for which to assume a continuing loss. This has to be a fairly arbitrary decision, because of the difficulty of estimating how long you will remain out of work.

There are three grounds on which the Tribunal may decide not to award even the full amount of the money which you have already lost. These grounds are:

(a) If you have made no reasonable efforts to find a new job, the compensation will be limited to the period for which you could have expected to be unemployed if you had made reasonable efforts.
(b) The Tribunal may decide that you have been unfairly dismissed, because of some procedural irregularity, but that you would have gone anyway a few weeks later if your employer had handled the matter properly. In that event, your compensation is likely to be limited to your losses for those few weeks. This could happen, for example, if you are off work through illness, with no prospect of being fit for work in the foreseeable future, but your employer dismisses you unfairly by failing first to consult you or ask you to attend for a medical examination.
(c) There is a maximum figure which can be awarded as the

compensatory award. The amount is usually increased at the beginning of April, but no increase was made at the beginning of April 1992. The current figure is £10,000.

In fixing the compensatory award, the Industrial Tribunal does not deduct anything for any unemployment benefit or supplementary benefit which you have received. However, if you have received benefit the Tribunal will notify the Department of Employment. The Department can serve notice on the employer to recoup the benefit out of your compensation, so that the employer then has to pay to you only the balance of the award after deducting the amount paid to the Department.

The other element of the compensation awarded is a fairly nominal payment to compensate you for the loss of the *statutory rights* which go with your job. The current figure commonly awarded is £100 or thereabouts.

The whole of the compensation awarded to you is meant to compensate you for the money which you have lost or are likely to lose through being dismissed. The Tribunal has no power to award you anything for injured feelings or the worry and distress of being unfairly dismissed.

The additional award

Additional compensation may be awarded if your case is one of the rare ones where the Tribunal orders your employer to reinstate or re-engage you. If your employer does not comply with the order, even though it is practicable for him to do so, you can go back to the Tribunal and ask it to make an additional award of compensation. In most cases, the award must be not less than 13 weeks' pay and not more than 26 weeks' pay. The amount of a week's pay is to be your actual gross pay or a maximum figure which is set from time to time by Parliament, whichever is the lower. The maximum as from 1 April 1992 is £205 per week. Accordingly, if your gross pay was £205 or more, the minimum additional award is £2,665 and the maximum is £5,330.

The additional award is increased if your dismissal involves sex discrimination or racial discrimination. Details of the compensation in such cases are given at the end of this chapter.

The additional award is not payable if you have been dismissed because of your trade union membership or activities or non-membership of a union. Instead, the *special award*, which is in any

Your Employment Rights

case substantial, can be increased. The special award is dealt with in Chapter 13.

Deductions and contributory fault

There are several grounds on which the Tribunal may reduce the amount of the compensation which would otherwise have been awarded to you. The most important of these grounds are as follows:

(a) The amount of any redundancy payment to you by your employer will be taken into account.
(b) The amount of any ex-gratia payment by your employer will also usually be taken into account.
(c) If you have been offered your job back (or a suitable alternative job) and have unreasonably refused, this could lead to the basic award and the compensatory award being reduced. Obviously in these circumstances the additional award (for failing to offer to take you back) cannot be payable at all.
(d) If you are 64 years of age on the effective date of your dismissal, the amount of the basic award will be reduced by one-twelfth for every complete month between the effective date of dismissal and your 64th birthday. These are known as the tapering provisions. If you are 65 or more at the effective date of dismissal, you cannot complain about unfair dismissal at all, as mentioned on page 60.
(e) Any part of the compensation can also be reduced by a proportion to reflect the extent of your own contribution to your dismissal. In practice, this question of contributory fault usually arises where the dismissal is on the ground of misconduct. If you have been guilty of serious misconduct but your employer has gone wrong on the procedure, so that the dismissal is technically unfair, it would be unreasonable for you to receive full compensation. In such circumstances, both the basic award and the compensatory award will be reduced (it is difficult to envisage either the additional award or the special award being made at all in these circumstances). In a bad case, your contribution could be put at 100 per cent, so that although there will be a finding of unfair dismissal in your favour you will actually receive no compensation at all.

Your Rights if you are Sacked

Racial and sex discrimination

The definitions of racial and sex discrimination have already been explained in Chapter 1 and Chapter 9. There could be a finding of discrimination if you are dismissed, for example, for misconduct or incapacity, in circumstances where an employee of a different colour or the opposite sex has been treated more leniently.

If you are victimised for some legitimate step which you have taken in relation to racial or sex discrimination or equal pay, you have the same rights as if there had been direct discrimination against you. An example would be if you were dismissed for making a equal pay claim (whether or not this claim succeeds, so long as it was made in good faith).

The amount of compensation which can be awarded for direct racial or sex discrimination is subject to a maximum figure which is the same as the maximum figure for the compensatory award in unfair dismissal cases. The current maximum is £10,000.

If your dismissal involves racial or sex discrimination it will almost certainly also be an unfair dismissal. You should accordingly bring a claim for unfair dismissal as well as sex or racial discrimination. This involves one single Tribunal application, but with both parts of the claim specified in it.

There are the following important differences between unfair dismissal and discrimination claims:

(a) Compensation for injured feelings can be awarded in discrimination cases, as part of the overall maximum award of £10,000.

(b) If the additional award becomes payable, because of the employer's failure to comply with a reinstatement or re-engagement order, the amount of this award is doubled in cases which also involve sex or racial discrimination. It will be recalled that in other cases the minimum amount of the additional award is 13 weeks' pay and the maximum is 26 weeks' pay (but with a ceiling, currently £205, on the amount of a week's pay). Where the dismissal involves racial or sex discrimination the minimum award is based on 26 weeks' pay and the maximum on 52 weeks' pay. Accordingly, if you earn £205 per week (gross) or more, the current minimum award is £5,330 and the maximum is £10,660.

(c) You may have the right to complain about sex or racial discrimination even if you do not have the right to complain about unfair dismissal; for example, because you have been employed for less than two years or are above normal retirement age. There are very few jobs where the law does not give a right to complain about discrimination in dismissing you (although there are special rules if you are a member of the armed forces). The only important general exception is the one relating to employment outside Great Britain (although jobs on some British ships and aircraft are included).

If the discrimination against you was indirect, no compensation will be awarded for the discrimination itself, so long as the employer can show that there was no intention to discriminate. However, if you also bring a successful unfair dismissal claim and the additional award becomes payable, the amount of this award is doubled whether the discrimination against you is direct or indirect.

Time limit
The time limit for complaining of unfair dismissal is only three months from the effective date of termination of your employment. If you are also complaining of discrimination, the time limit of three months usually runs from the date of the decision which you are complaining about.

Your employer's insolvency
If you succeed in a complaint of unfair dismissal but your employer does not pay because he is insolvent, you can apply to the Redundancy Payments Office for the basic award (but not the compensatory award or any other head of compensation) to be paid to you from the Redundancy Fund.

Outstanding wages
If, when you are dismissed, your employer owes you wages (including bonus or commission) or holiday pay, you can include a claim for this money, under the Wages Act, in your Tribunal application. There is a time limit of three months from the date when the money should have been paid, but the Tribunal has the power to extend the time limit on the ground that it was not reasonably practicable for you to comply with it.

If you are out of time for making a Tribunal application under

Your Rights if you are Sacked

the Wages Act, you will have to bring Court proceedings to recover the money as a debt. The time limit for these proceedings is six years.

You will also have to take your case to Court and not to an Industrial Tribunal if you are dismissed without due notice and you do not receive the appropriate payment in lieu of notice. Your claim is one for wrongful dismissal, as explained at the beginning of this chapter.

CHAPTER 11
Your Rights if you Walk Out

As a general rule, if you choose to leave your employment, you will not be entitled to any compensation from your employer. If you have given due notice, in accordance with the terms of your contract, you will be entitled to be paid up to the date when you leave and you may also be entitled to holiday pay, depending on the terms of your contract.

If you leave your job without giving due notice, so that you are in breach of contract, you may not even be entitled to recover any arrears of pay for the work which you have already done. If you have broken your contract with him, your employer can claim to offset, against any money owing to you, the amount of any loss or expense caused to him by your sudden departure. This whole question of your employer's rights against you is considered in more detail in Chapter 16.

What if you resign and then wish to change your mind? The general rule is that once your notice of termination has been given and accepted, it is too late for you to change your mind.

The same general rule applies if you and your employer have agreed that your employment should come to an end on a certain date. Having made the agreement, you cannot then go back on it. It does not matter whether it was you or your employer who first suggested that your employment should be terminated, so long as a genuine agreement has been reached. There are, however, three important exceptions to the general rule.

The first exception applies if you have resigned or agreed to leave under duress. If your employer makes it clear to you that you will be sacked if you do not resign or agree to go, and you have no choice in the matter, you have in reality been dismissed.

Second, there are exceptional circumstances in which what appeared to be a resignation on your part was not genuinely so intended and should not have been so understood by your employer. For example:

> You have a blazing row with your boss, in the course of which you say, 'Right, that's it, I'm off,' and storm out of the office. When you come back later that day you are told that your resignation has been accepted and that you must clear your desk, pick up your cards and go home. You would have a good chance, in a case such as this, of satisfying a Tribunal that you had not genuinely resigned and that your employer had dismissed you.

You should, nevertheless, try to avoid giving your employer any grounds for claiming that you have resigned. You should not say anything that could be treated as a resignation, however strongly you may feel. If you do say something of this kind or walk out, you should come back without delay and make it quite clear that you have not resigned. If you walk out and stay away, this staying away could be said to be a further indication of your intention to resign.

The third case in which a resignation may not be what it seems is where you leave but claim that you have been constructively dismissed. This question of constructive dismissal is a major question, to which the remainder of this chapter will be devoted.

Constructive dismissal

You have been constructively dismissed if both the following questions can be answered yes:

(a) Has your employer broken his contract with you?
(b) Is this breach of contract serious enough to justify you in treating yourself as dismissed?

It does not matter whether your employer has broken an expressly stated term of the contract or one which is implied by law, so long as there has been a clear breach of contract. If, on the other hand, your employer does something which is unreasonable or unfair, but within the terms of your contract, if you leave it will be a straightforward resignation and not dismissal. If your employer imposes a wage reduction or demotes you, these would generally be breaches of contract which would justify you in treating yourself as constructively dismissed. If you leave your employment in response to the employer's breach of contract, the effect will be as if you had been dismissed on the date of your

Your Rights if you Walk Out

resignation. You can then bring an Industrial Tribunal claim for unfair dismissal, so long as you do so within the three-month time limit.

Usually, the employer's breach of contract is less straightforward than this, particularly where it is an implied term of the contract, rather than an express term, which you believe to have been broken. In such cases, you as the employee are faced with the following dilemma:

(a) On the one hand, if you give up your job and bring a constructive dismissal claim, there is the risk that your claim may fail. The Industrial Tribunal may take the view that the employer has not broken the contract, or it may decide that the matter was not serious enough to justify you in leaving. You cannot then change your mind and go back to your job. You will have given up your job without receiving any compensation at all.

(b) On the other hand, if you do have the right to leave and bring a constructive dismissal claim, you may lose this right if you delay. Even a delay of a few weeks could be too long. If, for example, you are demoted but continue to go into work and do the new job, after a short time, weeks rather than months, you will be regarded as having in effect agreed to a change in your contract, so that you are now employed to do the inferior job. It will be too late for you to treat yourself as constructively dismissed.

If you are unhappy about a change or proposed change at work, you should take the following steps as a matter of urgency:

1. Complain to your employer immediately, make it clear that you are unhappy about the change or proposed change and ask your employer to reconsider. Pursue the matter actively through your employer's grievance procedure.
2. Find out whether what has been done or is proposed involves a breach of contract by the employer. This may mean taking legal advice on the matter. Some of the places where you can go for advice are suggested in Chapter 15.
3. Decide whether you are prepared to carry on working under the changed conditions. Would you prefer to accept the change in your contract rather than have to go out and find a new job? Would you be able to find a new job anyway? Or are

Your Employment Rights

you going to find work intolerable, particularly if, for example, you have been demoted?
4. If you are going to leave, leave quickly. If you have pursued the matter as an internal grievance, but your employer's decision stands, that is the time to go. Do not wait any longer.

The following are important matters which can give rise to considerable uncertainty:

(a) A change in your place of work.
(b) Matters which undermine your authority and show that your employer has lost confidence in you.
(c) Serious acts of racial or sex discrimination.

Each of these matters will be considered separately.

Your place of work

There are many jobs which necessarily involve travel. If, for example, you are a sales representative and it is your job to visit customers all over the country, you cannot complain about having to travel.

But what if you have become used to doing all your work in one particular factory, shop or office, perhaps for many years? Your employers want to transfer you to another branch which they have just acquired. If they insist on transferring you, giving you no choice in the matter, can you treat yourself as constructively dismissed?

There are three matters to be considered. Does your contract contain any relevant terms on this matter? If not, should any terms be implied? If transferred, would you still be living within reasonable travelling distance of home?

Broadly speaking, the answer is likely to be as follows, although it is necessary to look carefully at the circumstances of each individual case:

(a) If the new place of work is more than a reasonable travelling distance from home, so that you will have to move house or stay in lodgings, you can probably treat yourself as constructively dismissed, unless there is an express term in the contract under which your employers are entitled to transfer you.
(b) If you will still be working within reasonable travelling

Your Rights if you Walk Out

distance of home, you will probably not be entitled to treat yourself as constructively dismissed, unless there is something in your contract to prevent the transfer.

Lack of confidence in you

Not all the terms of your contract will be found written down, as was explained in Chapter 3. The law will imply terms which are necessary to make the contract work. One of the most important is the implied term of mutual trust and confidence. As the word 'mutual' indicates, this works both ways.

You for your part must not do anything which undermines your relationship with your employer. If, for example, you make it clear that you have no respect for your employer or your immediate boss and you openly refuse to obey the lawful and proper instructions which you are given, you are making your employer's position untenable and you cannot complain if you are dismissed.

At the same time, your employer will generally be in breach of contract if, without reasonable justification, he demonstrates that he no longer has trust and confidence in you and thereby makes it impossible for you to do your job properly. Most complaints of this kind involve senior employees. The following is an example of a case where you would probably be entitled to treat yourself as constructively dismissed:

> You are a senior and long-serving manager. Suddenly all your staff are told that they must not act on any of your instructions without having them confirmed by the managing director. You have given your employers no reasonable cause to take this step.

If you choose to walk out, you should be able to persuade a Court or Tribunal that you have been constructively dismissed.

Discrimination

If you are the victim of racial or sex discrimination at work, this does not automatically mean that you can walk out and treat yourself as constructively dismissed. Your employer can generally be held responsible in law for a single act of discrimination against you by a fellow employee, even if the employer personally and senior management are not aware of the discrimination, but in

Your Employment Rights

these circumstances you would not have a very good chance of succeeding in an unfair dismissal claim if you walked out.

There are, however, circumstances in which serious or persistent discrimination which drives you out of your job can lead to a successful unfair dismissal claim. For example:

> You are the personal secretary to the owner of a business. He makes sexual advances to you virtually every day, to the extent that you dread going into work. If you can stand this situation no longer and give up your job, you should succeed in an unfair dismissal claim, on the basis that you have been constructively dismissed.

Compensation

As already mentioned, the effect of a constructive dismissal is identical to that of an actual dismissal. You may be able to take Court proceedings for wrongful dismissal or Industrial Tribunal proceedings for unfair dismissal, depending on the circumstances.

You will have a right to claim damages for wrongful dismissal if you are employed under a contract for a fixed term and you leave before this term has expired. You could also have this right if you do not have a fixed-term contract but you have left without giving notice. The rules for calculating the compensation, or damages, were explained in Chapter 10.

More usually, a constructive dismissal leads to a claim for unfair dismissal. However, it is important to bear in mind that you can bring an unfair dismissal claim only if you can satisfy the various conditions which were explained in Chapter 10. In particular, you need to have two years' continuous employment up to the date of termination of your employment (or five years' if you worked for eight or more hours per week but less than 16 hours).

If you succeed in an unfair dismissal claim, the rules for fixing the compensation will be identical to those which were explained in Chapter 10. Indeed, the law does not use the expression 'constructive dismissal' at all. No distinction is made between a constructive dismissal and an actual dismissal. The only question is whether the dismissal is unfair.

If you have been constructively dismissed by reason of serious racial or sex discrimination against you, it is important that your Tribunal application should mention both complaints. You should refer both to unfair dismissal and to sex (or racial) discrimination. If you succeed in your discrimination claim, as well or instead of

Your Rights if you Walk Out

your unfair dismissal claim, you will be entitled to compensation for injured feelings as well as compensation for your financial losses.

CHAPTER 12

Your Rights if you are Made Redundant

To say that you are made redundant is a short way of saying that you are dismissed on account of redundancy.

What is redundancy?

There is a redundancy if your employer anticipates, or already has, a need for fewer employees, either generally or to do some particular kind of work. The effect of the redundancy may be felt either throughout your employer's operations or at one or more particular factories or shops or other establishments.

A redundancy could come about for a number of reasons. For example:

(a) There has been a downturn in business and your employer needs to cut costs by reducing the number of employees.
(b) A whole factory or plant which is doing badly is closed down.
(c) A general slimming down in the business results in a need for fewer office staff.
(d) New technology or automation or computerisation means that fewer employees are required.
(e) A particular activity which has until now been carried out by employees is contracted out to a separate company. This could be part of the manufacturing process or it could be some ancillary activity such as cleaning or security.

If you are dismissed on the ground of redundancy, this could be for any of the following reasons:

(a) All the jobs at your factory or other establishment are going.
(b) Your employer no longer needs any employees at all to do the work which you are doing; for example, if you are a security guard and the whole of that function is being contracted out.

Your Employment Rights

(c) Your employer needs a reduced number of employees to do your kind of work and you are selected for redundancy.
(d) The job of a fellow employee is to disappear and that employee is transferred to your job, perhaps because he or she has longer service than you, and you are then made redundant.

Your rights if made redundant

If you are dismissed on account of redundancy, you could have one of five rights:

(a) The right to claim a redundancy payment.
(b) The right to claim that you have been unfairly dismissed.
(c) The right to time off to look for other work.
(d) The right to complain of racial or sex discrimination.
(e) A claim to equal pay.

Each of these rights will now be explained in turn. You should note that you may not have all the above rights, particularly (a) and (b). For example, you may not have long enough continuous service. Remember that your continuous service may go back to before the date when you started with your present employer. If the business has changed hands, your continuous service will generally run from the date when you started work for the previous owner of the business. There could indeed have been several changes of ownership, with your continuity of employment being preserved each time.

Your right to a redundancy payment

One of the most important conditions for a redundancy payment is length of service. You will not be entitled to a payment if you had less than two years' continuous service at the relevant date. Usually the relevant date is the date on which your employment comes to an end, whether by notice or without notice. There is, however, one special provision. If you are dismissed without notice less than a week before you have two years' continuous service, it would be unfair if your employer, by acting wrongfully in this way, could deprive you of the right to claim a redundancy payment. In these circumstances, therefore, the relevant date is the date on which a week's notice would have expired if that notice had been given.

Generally, if you are a part-time employee, working less than 16

Your Rights if you are Made Redundant

hours a week, you will not be entitled to redundancy payment unless you have been continuously employed for five years at the relevant date. If you work less than eight hours a week, you will not be entitled to a payment at all, however long you have been employed. There are, however, special and rather complicated rules to cover cases where you have at some stage during your employment worked eight or more hours or 16 or more hours (as the case may be).

You can also lose the right to a redundancy payment when you reach a certain age. If there is a normal retiring age in your employer's business for employees doing the kind of job which you do (say the age of 60), you will not be entitled to a redundancy payment if on the relevant date you are above that age. Whether or not there is a normal retiring age, you will not have the right to a payment if on the relevant date you are 65. Until a few years ago there were different ages for men and women (65 and 60 respectively), but now the age is 65 for both.

You may also be excluded from the right to a redundancy payment because of the kind of job you do. The main jobs excluded are:

(a) Most jobs outside Great Britain. You will only have the right if you ordinarily work in Great Britain or if on the relevant date you are in Great Britain in accordance with your employer's instructions. There are special rules for British ships and offshore installations.
(b) Civil servants and public employees. You are excluded if you are a civil servant or member of the armed forces. You may also be excluded if you are employed in a public office. If you are a civil servant or other public servant you may have your own scheme, however.
(c) Share fishermen. You are excluded if you are the master or member of the crew of a fishing vessel and your only remuneration is a share in the profits or gross earnings.
(d) Employees of an overseas government.
(e) Certain domestic servants. You are excluded if you are employed in a private household by a close relative.

Voluntary exclusions

There is only one possibility of making a binding agreement to exclude your rights to a redundancy payment. This is as follows:

Your Employment Rights

You are employed under a contract for a fixed term of two years or more. The contract excludes your right to a redundancy payment if your contract is not renewed. You will not be able to claim a redundancy payment if your contract expires and your employer does not renew it.

You could also lose your right to a redundancy payment if your union has entered into a collective agreement containing redundancy provisions for your benefit. So long as the provisions are at least as satisfactory as those in the statutory scheme, the Secretary of State for Employment can make an exemption order. In that event you will not be able to claim under the statutory scheme. This should not matter because you should do at least as well under the voluntary scheme.

Voluntary redundancy

If your employer states that there are to be redundancies and asks for volunteers, you should still be entitled to a redundancy payment if you volunteer. It is different, however, if it is your own idea to leave. You will not be entitled to a redundancy payment if you give up your job and look for a new one when you learn that you are likely to be made redundant.

Alternative employment

You may also lose your right to a redundancy payment if your employer offers you alternative employment and you refuse. There are two possibilities. In the first case:

(a) Your employer offers you a new job before your redundancy takes effect.
(b) The new job is to start when the old one ends or within four weeks afterwards.
(c) You will be doing the same kind of work as before, at the same place and on the same terms and conditions.

Unless you have reasonable grounds for refusing the offer (which is unlikely), you must either accept the offer or lose your right to a redundancy payment.

The other possibility is that you receive a similar offer to that described above, but there is some difference between the new job and the old job in relation to the kind of work, the place of work or the terms and conditions of employment. If you turn the new job down you will lose your right to a redundancy payment only if the

Your Rights if you are Made Redundant

new job would have been suitable (viewed from all aspects) and if you have acted unreasonably in turning it down.

You have an alternative course of action, however. If you take the new job, you have a trial period which runs until four weeks after you started. If you terminate the contract during this period, and do so on reasonable grounds, you will be entitled to a redundancy payment as if the alternative employment had never been offered to you.

The amount of the redundancy payment

The calculation of the redundancy payment involves what can be rather complicated arithmetic.

The first stage is to establish the amount of a week's pay. Your pay for this purpose includes both your basic pay and also any bonus or commission which you are entitled to under the terms of your contract. If your pay varies, an average figure for the last 12 months of your employment is taken. There is a maximum figure, which on 1 April 1992 went up from £198 to £205.

The next stage is to arrive at a number of years by counting back from the relevant date (usually the date on which your employment comes to an end). You must count back to arrive at the shortest of the following periods:

(a) The period during which you have been continuously employed. Remember that you may be able to count service in the business with a previous employer if the business has changed hands.
(b) The period since your 18th birthday.
(c) The last 20 years.

Your redundancy pay is one week's gross wage (up to the maximum of £205) for every complete year in the above period, but with an increase to 1½ weeks' pay for every year throughout which you were 41 or more and a reduction to half a week's pay for any year in part of which you were below the age of 22.

For example:

> You are 48 and have worked continuously for the last six years, earning £300 per week. Your redundancy payment will be the maximum week's wage of £205 multiplied by 9 (1½ for each continuous year's service above the age of 41), which produces a figure of £1,845.

Your Employment Rights

When I'm 64

If you are 65 at the relevant date, you will not be entitled to a redundancy payment at all. If you are 64, the payment is reduced by one-twelfth for each month after your 64th birthday.

Your employer's insolvency
If your employer is insolvent, you can apply to the Redundancy Payments Office for payment out of the Redundancy Fund.

Tribunal claims
If your claim to a redundancy payment is disputed or your employer fails to pay you, you can refer the matter to an Industrial Tribunal. You must submit your Tribunal application within six months after the relevant date (usually the last day of your employment).

When you are dismissed, there is a presumption by law that you have been dismissed on account of redundancy unless your employer proves otherwise.

Unfair dismissal

Dismissal on account of redundancy can also be an unfair dismissal, so you can then bring a claim of the kind described in Chapter 10. Some dismissals on account of redundancy are automatically unfair. These include selection for redundancy on account of pregnancy, as explained in Chapter 5.

There are also two circumstances in which your dismissal could be automatically unfair where you are selected for redundancy and one or more other employees in the same undertaking and in a similar position to you are not selected. Your dismissal is automatically unfair if:

(a) You have been selected because of your trade union membership or activities or because you are not a member of a union.
(b) Your selection for redundancy was in contravention of some customary arrangement or agreed procedure (which will usually be contained in a collective agreement with your union).

Your right to bring a claim for unfair dismissal in the above circumstances will only arise if the conditions explained in

Chapter 10 are all met, including your two years' continuous service up to the effective date of termination of your employment. The same rule applies in the other cases of unfair dismissal mentioned below.

If your selection for redundancy is not automatically unfair, you may nevertheless be able to bring a claim if your employer has acted unreasonably either in selecting you for redundancy or in the way in which the redundancy was handled. You can expect to succeed in a claim for unfair dismissal if your employer handles the redundancy in a harsh and insensitive way; for example, by telling you that you are redundant and dismissing you on the spot, without any kind of consultation. You will also generally have been unfairly dismissed if your employer has not given adequate consideration to the possibility of offering you some alternative employment.

The principles relating to compensation for unfair dismissal were set out in Chapter 10.

Time off

When you are given notice on account of redundancy, you will be entitled to paid time off so long as you will have been continuously employed for two years or more on the date on which the notice is due to expire (or would expire if you had been given the minimum notice to which you are entitled by law). If you work at least eight hours a week but fewer than 16 hours you will need five years' continuous employment. You will also not have the right if you ordinarily work outside Great Britain under your contract of employment or if you are employed as a merchant seaman or as a share fisherman or in the police service.

If you do have the right, you may take reasonable time off during your working hours to look for new employment or to make arrangements for training for future employment.

If your employer refuses to allow you the time off, you have the right to take your case to an Industrial Tribunal. You must submit the application within three months after your request for time off was refused. The Tribunal may award compensation of up to two-fifths of a week's pay (ie usually two days' pay).

Your Employment Rights

Discrimination

Your selection for redundancy may involve racial or sex discrimination. For example:

> You are a woman working part time at a factory. You have worked there for 20 years. The company are selecting employees to be made redundant and they decide to dismiss all the part-time workers first. Many of the women in the factory but hardly any of the men work part time. You are made redundant, even though men who work full time but have only a couple of years' service are kept on. This could be indirect sex discrimination against you.

Where a dismissal is discriminatory it will usually also be an unfair dismissal. In presenting an application to an Industrial Tribunal you should state that you are complaining about both sex discrimination and unfair dismissal. The maximum award in unfair dismissal cases can be greater than in sex discrimination cases (because any basic award and additional award are on top of the compensatory award), but the compensation for discrimination can include a figure for injured feelings. Your Tribunal application should be submitted within three months after the date of the decision to dismiss you.

Equal pay

It has now been established by the European Court that any money which you receive in connection with your redundancy counts as pay for the purposes of the equal pay provisions of Community law. It does not matter whether the money which you receive is paid under a statutory scheme or under your contract or under some voluntary arrangements by the employer. It does not matter either whether it is described as redundancy pay or as a severance payment or as a termination payment. You could have an equal pay claim if one or more comparable employees of the opposite sex receive more than you do.

CHAPTER 13
Your Rights as a Trade Union Member (or Non-member)

Some of the rights which you have as a trade union member have already been explained in earlier chapters. These rights include:

(a) Your right not to be turned down for a job because of your trade union membership (Chapter 1).
(b) Your right not to be selected for redundancy on account of your trade union membership (Chapter 12).

You have corresponding rights if you are treated in either of the above ways because you do not belong to a union.

Your other very important right is your right not to be dismissed because of your trade union membership or activities or non-membership. There are several associated rights and benefits if you are dismissed for one of these reasons.

There is then a separate right not to be subjected to pressure short of dismissal for one of these reasons.

You also have a right to paid leave if you are a safety representative appointed by a recognised trade union (Chapter 4).

You have this right to time off work in two further cases, which are explained at the end of this chapter.

Dismissal for union membership, activities or non-membership

You have the right not to be dismissed because:

(a) You are a member of an independent trade union or propose to join one.
(b) You have taken part or proposed to take part in the activities of an independent trade union.

Your Employment Rights

(c) You are not a trade union member or a member of some particular trade union.
(d) You refused to join or become a member or said that you were going to refuse.

The reference in (b) to trade union activities means activities outside your working hours or activities which are permissible in accordance with arrangements agreed with your employer or consent given by him.

These rights are enjoyed by all employees who have the right not to be unfairly dismissed, with two important additions. You have the above rights even if you have been continuously employed for less than two years (even for only one day). You also have them if you have carried on working beyond normal retirement age.

Furthermore, if you are dismissed for any of the above reasons the dismissal is automatically unfair.

There are a number of respects in which the *compensation* payable to you will be increased if you are dismissed for one of the above reasons.

First of all, you will be entitled to a *special award* of compensation. The amount of the special award is based on your actual week's pay (without the £205.00 upper limit), but with a minimum and maximum figure. These minimum and maximum figures are increased every year or every other year, usually on 1 April. The current annual figures, with effect from 1 April 1992, are £13,400 and £26,800. Accordingly the amount of the special award cannot be less than £13,400.

There is one important condition to be met before a special award of compensation can be awarded. You will not be entitled to the award unless you have applied to the Tribunal for reinstatement or re-engagement. It is therefore vitally important that you should make this application.

Secondly, if the Industrial Tribunal orders your employer to re-employ you or re-engage you and the employer refuses to comply, the special award will go up. The special award goes up to £20,100 or 106 weeks' pay, whichever is the greater, with no maximum figure. In these cases the special award replaces the additional award which was explained in Chapter 10.

Thirdly, there is a minimum figure for the basic award. The current figure is £2,700.

Your Rights as a Trade Union Member (or Non-member)

You have a further important right. You can apply for *interim relief* as long as you can comply with a strict time limit (only seven days for your Tribunal application to be received) and other strict rules. The procedure is explained in Chapter 15. The interim relief consists of an order for your employer to reinstate you until your claim for unfair dismissal can be heard.

Industrial action

It will be seen that you have extensive rights if you are dismissed for taking part in the activities of an independent trade union, as long as these are agreed activities or they take place outside working hours.

On the other hand, you will generally be in a very weak position if you are dismissed while taking part in a strike or other industrial action or during a lock-out.

If the action is *official*, your dismissal will be automatically fair, so long as you are dismissed while still taking part in the action and as long as your employer does not act selectively. He or she must not sack you while keeping on any of the others who are involved. He will also be acting selectively if he sacks one or more of the others and then takes them back again within three months.

If the industrial action is *unofficial*, your position is even worse. Your dismissal while taking part in the action will be automatically lawful even if your employer acts selectively.

Pressure short of dismissal

If you have the above rights (for example if you are not in the police service) you also have the right not to be subjected by your employer to pressure to cause you to leave the union or not to join. You also have a similar right as a non-union member not to be subjected to pressure to make you join a union or stop you leaving.

An example of the sort of pressure which would be unlawful is refusing to increase your pay in line with that of other employees unless you agree to leave the union.

If you are subjected to unlawful pressure you can take your case to an Industrial Tribunal within three months. There is no limit on the compensation which can be awarded.

Your Employment Rights
Time off

If you are a member of a union recognised by your employer, you have the right to time off for certain union activities. Examples of the permitted activities are attendance at an executive committee meeting or annual conference. You are not, however, permitted to take time off in order to take part in a strike or other industrial action.

The time taken and the purposes for which it is taken must be reasonable. There is a Code of Practice.

Although you are entitled to leave in the above circumstances, this is *unpaid* leave.

If the leave which you have requested is unreasonably refused, then you can complain to an Industrial Tribunal within three months and the Tribunal, if your claim is upheld, can award compensation.

The second right to time off is one which you enjoy only if you are an official of a union recognised by your employer. This term 'official' includes branch officers and shop stewards.

The purposes for which time off can be requested include a number of matters in connection with your duties as a union official, for example, negotiations with the employer, informing members about the negotiations and consulting them and representing members in disciplinary matters. You are also entitled to time off to attend a relevant course on industrial relations which has been approved by the TUC or by your own union.

Again, the requirement is that you be given such time off as is reasonable in the circumstances and again there is a Code of Practice. If you are unreasonably refused time off, you can complain to an Industrial Tribunal which can award compensation.

This right to time off is different from your rights as an ordinary union member mentioned above in one very important respect. You are entitled to *paid* leave.

Both your rights to time off are subject to some exceptions. You do not have the right if you ordinarily work outside Great Britain under your contract of employment of if you are employed in the police service or as a share fisherman or if you normally work less than 16 hours a week.

CHAPTER 14
Your Rights as an Ex-employee

After you have ceased to be an employee you may still have some rights against your employer, quite apart from your right to complain of unfair dismissal or to claim a redundancy payment. The most important of these matters relates to your pension, but you could also have rights in relation to continuing fringe benefits or references.

Pensions

Your employer is not obliged to provide or contribute to a pension for you, unless there is a term in your contract to that effect. If a pension is provided, however, you have certain rights. One of the most important of these rights arises if you change jobs before retiring. You are entitled to have the transfer value of your pension paid to your new employer's pension fund or to a personal pension fund.

It is now established that any pension which you receive is treated as pay for the purposes of the equal pay provisions of Community law. This means that any future pension provision for you by your employer must not treat you less favourably than comparable employees of the opposite sex.

It is not yet certain how far the important decision of the European Court on these matters has retrospective effect. Millions of employees are receiving or will be receiving pensions which are based wholly or in part on contributions made by their employers before May 1990, when the European Court gave its ruling on this matter. The question which has not yet been established is whether it is only pension arrangements and employers' contributions which must be non-discriminatory with effect from May 1990, or whether all pension payments themselves must be made on a basis of equality as from that date.

Your Employment Rights

The latter approach would cost the employers and pension funds billions of pounds and is unlikely to be adopted.

One thing is certain, however. If you join a scheme in the future (for example, on changing jobs) or have joined since 23 May 1990, you must be treated equally with comparable employees of the opposite sex in the following respects:

(a) The contributions payable by you and your employer.
(b) The date at which you can start drawing your pension.
(c) Any provisions for early retirement on pension.
(d) The amount (or basis of calculation) of the pension.
(e) Benefits for dependants.

If you have a complaint about the way in which your pension scheme is being administered or about the way in which your own rights are being disregarded you should complain to the Pensions Ombudsman, Mr Michael Platt, at 11 Belgrave Road, London SW1E 1RB (Phone 071-834 9144).

Discrimination in fringe benefits

It is possible that your former employer will continue to allow you fringe benefits after you have retired. There must be no sex or racial discrimination in the way in which such benefits are provided. For example:

> You have retired from service with a bus company. You are still allowed to enjoy free travel, but your husband is not. The concession is given not only to former male employees but also to their wives. This sex discrimination against you is unlawful and you could take your case to an Industrial Tribunal.

References

As a general rule, your former employer is under no obligation to give you a reference (although there may be isolated cases where former employers are under a contractual or statutory duty to do so). If, however, a reference is given, there are two possible claims which you could have if the reference is inaccurate and damaging to you.

You could bring proceedings in the Courts for negligence, if your employer has been careless in giving the reference and you

Your Rights as an Ex-employee

lose or fail to obtain a new job as a result. For example, he may have been negligent in failing to give the matter adequate thought or consult the members of management who knew you personally or look at the relevant records.

You may also be able to bring proceedings for defamation (libel or slander) if any written or spoken reference given by your employer is inaccurate and damaging to you and if your employer does this from motives of malice (in the legal sense of the word). If your employer gives a reference which he knows to be untrue you could be successful in a claim against him.

Legal aid is available to bring proceedings for negligence (subject to your income and capital being low enough) but not for defamation.

CHAPTER 15
Claiming Your Rights

A great many of the rights described in this book can be enforced by Industrial Tribunal proceedings. The most important of these rights are those relating to:

(a) Unfair dismissal
(b) Redundancy pay
(c) Equal pay
(d) Racial and sex discrimination
(e) Discrimination against you for your trade union membership or activities or non-membership
(f) Your right to return to work after pregnancy.

If your employer fails to pay wages which are due to you then you can generally either make a Tribunal claim under the Wages Act or sue your employer in the County Court for payment of the debt. There are other claims which you can pursue only through the Courts. The most important of these are claims for wrongful dismissal (Chapters 10 and 11) and claims if you are injured at work (Chapter 7).

Claims to Statutory Maternity Pay fall into a special category. If your employer does not pay what is due to you, then you should refer the matter to the Department of Social Security and ask for a formal decision from the Adjudication Officer there. Ultimately, if your employer fails to pay what is due, he can be prosecuted for a criminal offence.

The purpose of this Chapter is to outline what is involved in taking your case to an Industrial Tribunal. The chapter does not explain how to bring Court proceedings for wrongful dismissal, unpaid wages or injuries at work. However the next section of this chapter, on help with your case, is relevant to Court proceedings as well. You may also be able to obtain legal aid for bringing Court proceedings, as long as your income and capital are below

Your Employment Rights

the very low limits which have been set. You cannot, on the other hand, obtain legal aid for representation at an Industrial Tribunal hearing.

Help with your case

Although legal aid is not available for Industrial Tribunal proceedings, there are several places where you may be able to go to obtain advice and help with your case. You may also be able to obtain free representation at the hearing. It will generally be an advantage to you to have legal representation, although if you do have to present your own case the Chairman of the Tribunal will try to put you at your ease and help you on points of law and procedure.

You may be able to obtain advice and assistance and perhaps also representation at the hearing:

(a) From a *solicitor*. If you cannot afford to pay, you may be able to obtain free advice (but not representation at the hearing) under what is known as the 'green form' scheme. When you speak to the solicitor, you should find out at the start whether he is in this scheme and whether you will qualify for the free advice.

(b) From the *Equal Opportunities Commission* (EOC) if you wish to complain about sex discrimination or bring an equal pay claim. The address and telephone number of the main office of the EOC are:
Equal Opportunities Commission
Overseas House
Quay Street
Manchester M3 3HN
(Phone 061-833 9244)

The EOC also has offices in Glasgow and Cardiff.

(c) From *The Commission for Racial Equality* (CRE) if you wish to complain about racial discrimination. The address and telephone number of the head office of the CRE are:
Commission for Racial Equality
Elliot House
10 - 12 Allington Street
London SW1E 5EH
(Phone 071-828 7022)

Claiming Your Rights

The CRE also has offices in Edinburgh, Manchester, Birmingham, Leeds and Leicester.

(d) From your *union*, if you belong to one.
(e) From a *Law Centre*, if there is one in your area. You should look in your local telephone directory, under 'Law Centres', to find out if there are any listed.
(f) From a *Citizens' Advice Bureau (CAB)*. To find the address of the nearest CAB you should look in your telephone directory under 'Citizens' Advice Bureaux'. Some CABs have specialist volunteers who may be prepared to take on your case and represent you at the hearing.

You should seek advice and assistance without delay, particularly if you are proposing to apply for assistance to the EOC, the CRE or your union, since it will usually take at least several weeks for your application to be dealt with.

Time Limits

It is of the greatest possible importance that you should comply with the time limit for submitting your Tribunal application. The time limits are very short and very strict. It is only in the most exceptional circumstances that they can be extended. The following are examples of the very short time limits which you must comply with:

(a) Three months from the effective date of termination of your employment, if you are complaining about unfair dismissal.
(b) Three months from the date of the decision not to employ you, if you are complaining that a prospective employer has refused to employ you because of your trade union membership or activities or non-membership of a union.
(c) Three months from the date of the act which you are complaining about, if your case relates to racial or sex discrimination.
(d) Seven days from the effective date of termination of your employment, if you wish to apply for interim relief, in a case where you are complaining that you have been dismissed because of your trade union membership or activities or your non-membership of a union.
(e) Six months from the 'relevant date' (usually the date on which

Your Employment Rights

your employment comes to an end), if you wish to apply for a redundancy payment.

You must not let the last date go by simply because you are waiting to find out more about the case or because you have applied to the CRE or EOC for assistance and are waiting for the outcome. You must not delay because you are pursuing your case through an internal grievance or appeal procedure.

Starting your case

To apply to have your case heard by an Industrial Tribunal, there are three things you should do:

(a) Obtain the form of Originating Application, known as the IT1.
(b) Fill the form in.
(c) Send it to the Central Office of Industrial Tribunals.

You can obtain the form from an Employment Office, Jobcentre or Unemployment Benefit Office. You should note the following points when you are filling in the form:

(a) Question 1 asks you to state the type of complaint. Remember that you may have more than one type of complaint, for example sex discrimination and equal pay, racial discrimination and unfair dismissal or redundancy and unpaid wages. If you are not sure about a claim, include it. It is easier to drop one of your claims later than to add a claim which you have missed out.

(b) You have to state the name and address of the employer or other person whom you are complaining about (the respondent). There may be more than one respondent. For example, if you wish to complain about sexual harassment by a colleague at work then you should name this colleague as respondent, as well as your employer.

(c) Question 10 requires you to give full details of your complaint. You should give enough information to make it clear what you are complaining about. If you are complaining about sexual harassment, for example, you should give details of each incident or as many as you can remember. If the space on the form is insufficient, you can continue on a separate sheet.

(d) If you are complaining of unfair dismissal, question 11 asks you to tick one or more of three boxes to show what remedy

Claiming Your Rights

you are seeking – reinstatement or re-engagement or compensation. Unless you already have a new job or there is absolutely no possibility that you would ever wish to go back you should tick all the three boxes. You cannot become eligible for the additional award of compensation (Chapter 10) or the special award (Chapter 13) unless reinstatement or re-engagement has been requested.

Having filled in the form, you must then send it to the Central Office of Industrial Tribunals in time to make sure that it arrives there within the time limit. Do not wait until the last possible day before sending the form. Try to send it at least a week or so before the time limit expires.

If you worked (or applied for a job) in England or Wales, you should send the completed form to:

Central Office of Industrial Tribunals
Southgate Street
Bury St Edmunds
Suffolk IP33 2AQ
(Phone 0284 762300)

If you worked (or applied for a job) in Scotland you should send the form to:

Central Office of Industrial Tribunals
St Andrews House
141 West Nile Street
Glasgow G1 2RU
(Phone 041-331 1601)

Applications for interim relief

An application for interim relief could arise if you believe that you have been dismissed on account of your trade union membership or activities or your non-membership of a union. You must submit the application without delay, so that it will be received at the Central Office of Industrial Tribunals within seven days of the effective date of termination of your employment.

If you are complaining that your dismissal is on account of your trade union membership or activities, a further document must be received at the Central Office within the seven-day period. The document required is a written certificate, signed by an authorised official of your union, stating that:

Your Employment Rights

(a) On the date when you were dismissed you were a member of the union or were proposing to become a member.
(b) There appear to be reasonable grounds for supposing that the reason (or principal reason) for your dismissal was the reason alleged in your Originating Application (ie trade union membership or activities).

It is particularly important, therefore, in this kind of case that you consult your union immediately after your dismissal, so that the certificate can be obtained and lodged in time.

Preliminary and procedural hearings

There are four kinds of Tribunal hearings or discussions which could take place before the full hearing of your case. These are as follows:

(a) A *pre-hearing assessment*. No evidence is heard at this stage. You (or your representative) will explain briefly what your case is about and why you have a good claim. The respondent will then reply. If the Tribunal come to the view that your case is unlikely to succeed, then you may be given what is commonly referred to as a 'costs warning'. You are entitled to proceed with your case, but you will be at risk of being ordered to pay the respondent's legal costs if you lose.
(b) A *pre-hearing discussion*. Again, no evidence is heard at this stage. The purpose is to clarify the issues, find out how many witnesses will be called and estimate how long the case will last.
(c) *An interlocutory hearing*. Again, generally, no evidence is heard. The purpose is to resolve disputes over procedure, for example whether the respondent should be ordered to produce documents which you need to see in order to help prove your case.
(d) A *preliminary hearing*, at which evidence may be called. This hearing may be needed in order to establish whether the Tribunal will have jurisdiction to hear your claim at all. For example, the respondent's Notice of Appearance (the document setting out the respondent's defence to your claim) may raise the question whether you are to be treated as an employee for the purposes of the relevant legislation. Even if you are technically self-employed the law may regard you as

Claiming Your Rights

an employee for the purpose of many of the rights explained in this book. This is particularly so in discrimination cases but it is true also of other complaints, including unfair dismissal. A preliminary hearing is also commonly arranged if your claim is out of time. The purpose of the preliminary hearing is to consider whether there are exceptional circumstances which justify extending the time limit. If you are claiming that you were not aware of the facts or law which gave rise to your claim, one matter to be taken into account will be how quickly you acted once you became aware of your rights.

Conciliation

Copies of your IT1 and the respondent's Notice of Appearance will be sent to an ACAS Conciliation Officer. He or she will speak both to you and the respondent (or your respective representatives) to explore the possibility of settling your claim. Things which are said by you to the Conciliation Officer or by him or her to you cannot be repeated at the Tribunal hearing. If a settlement is achieved this will be recorded on a form, known as a COT3, to be signed by both parties. The settlement will then be final and binding.

Preparing your case

(a) If you are complaining about racial or sex discrimination, remember the *questionnaire* procedure which was explained in Chapter 1. You should ask for advice from the CRE or EOC (as the case may be) about filling in the form, since sometimes it may be appropriate to ask a great many questions. You may submit the questions at the same time as the IT1 or before then, but you must in any event submit them within 21 days after the IT1 if you wish to be able to rely at all on the employer's failure to answer the questions properly.

(b) When you receive a copy of the respondent's Notice of Appearance, you can write to the respondent asking for *further particulars*. For example, if you have an unfair dismissal claim and your employer states that you were dismissed for incompetence, you will need details of the allegations of incompetence so that you can be prepared to deal with them at the hearing. If the information is not forthcoming within a reasonable time, then you should write to the Tribunal Office to ask for the respondent to be ordered to give the information. In the same way the respondent can ask for further particulars of your Originating Application (the IT1).

(c) You may wish to *amend* the IT1. One example would be where the form states that you are complaining of sex discrimination but the facts set out would also justify a complaint of unfair dismissal. If there is a pre-hearing discussion you can ask the Tribunal at this stage for leave to amend your claim. Otherwise, you should initially write to the Tribunal Office to explain how you wish to amend your claim and why. The matter is generally then dealt with by correspondence and leave is either given or refused. You can raise the question of amending your claim at the hearing itself, but it is far better to do so at an earlier stage. The respondent can also apply for leave to amend the Notice of Appearance.

(d) If you have any *relevant documents* you must take them with you to the Tribunal hearing. In most cases, the respondent is more likely than you are to have documents you need. If, for example, you are complaining about discrimination in not appointing you to a job, the relevant documents could include all the application forms and the interview notes. You should write to the respondent at an early stage asking for the documents to be made available to you for inspection (or for copies to be supplied) and produced at the hearing. If the respondent refuses or fails to answer you can then write to the Tribunal Office to explain what the documents are and why they are required and to ask for an Order for the documents to be produced.

(e) If you need evidence from some other person to help prove your case, then you should call that person as a *witness* on your behalf at the hearing. Although the Tribunal can look at a signed statement instead, this carries much less weight (and sometimes no weight at all).

If a witness is important to your case and there is any doubt at all about the witness attending (or being able to obtain time off work), you should apply to the Tribunal Office for a witness order. You should do this by sending a letter to the Tribunal Office, giving the name and address of the witness and saying why the evidence is relevant. If a witness order is

Claiming Your Rights

obtained, you must then hand the witness order to your witness or send it by registered or recorded delivery post.
(f) If you wish to ask for a *postponement*, for example because you or one of your witnesses are ill, then you should do so at the earliest possible date. If you fail to act promptly, or if you apply for postponement without good cause, then the postponement may be refused or you may be ordered to pay the legal costs and expenses which have been unnecessarily incurred by the respondent.

The hearing and the decision

If you are complaining of unfair dismissal and it is admitted that you were dismissed, then the employer's witnesses will give evidence first. In most other cases, your evidence and that of your witnesses will be heard first.

The respondent (or his representative) will have the right to question you and any other witness who gives evidence on your behalf. The Chairman and Members of the Tribunal may also ask questions. You in turn (or your representative) will have the right to question each of the respondent's witnesses after he or she has given evidence.

After all the evidence has been heard, you (or your representative) have the right to make a closing statement to the Tribunal, stating why the Tribunal should find in your favour in the light of the evidence which has been given. The respondent (or his representative) has a similar right. If you and your witnesses gave evidence first then you or your representative will have the last word. If the respondent's witnesses gave evidence first then it is the respondent (or his representative) who will speak last.

The Tribunal will either give a decision on the day or 'reserve' the decision. In either case, the decision will be set out in writing and sent to you through the post. If there is a finding in your favour, that finding and the question of compensation (or other remedy) may be dealt with at the same hearing or there may have to be a separate hearing to deal with the question of compensation.

You should in any event bring to the hearing all relevant documents, such as wage slips and details of job applications. You should also have worked out and written down beforehand any relevant figures, such as the amounts of your earnings and State

Your Employment Rights

Benefits since you lost your job, so that you can give the information to the Tribunal.

As a general rule, you will not be awarded *costs* if you win your case and you will not have to pay the respondent's costs if you lose. Costs could, however, be awarded against you in the following circumstances:

(a) If you acted unreasonably in taking your case to a Tribunal hearing, particularly if a 'costs warning' was made against you at a pre-hearing assessment.

(b) If you have put the respondent to unnecessary expense by causing a postponement of an earlier hearing or giving inadequate notice of your intention to ask for a postponement.

The respondent could also be ordered to pay costs if he is at fault in either of the above respects. There is also one special case. If you are complaining of unfair dismissal and have applied for reinstatement or re-engagement, the respondent must be ready with evidence to show whether your old job is still available. If the hearing has to be postponed, because the evidence is not available, and the respondent has no reasonable excuse, then the respondent can be order to pay the costs thrown away.

Whether you win or lose your case, you and your witnesses will be entitled to *expenses* for travelling, subsistence and loss of earnings. There are maximum amounts which can be awarded. You will be able to obtain details and the application form from the Clerk at the Tribunal hearing.

Appealing

The unsuccessful party, whether you or the respondent, can appeal to the Employment Appeal Tribunal on the ground that the Industrial Tribunal has gone wrong in law. The appeal must be lodged within 42 days from the date stamped at the end of the Tribunal decision. The period of 42 days runs from this date, not from the date when you actually receive the decision.

You may well need legal advice on the grounds for appeal. Various places where you can go for help are mentioned near the beginning of this chapter. In addition, legal aid is available for submitting or contesting an appeal to the Employment Appeal

Tribunal, even though it is not available for the Industrial Tribunal hearing.

You can lodge an appeal only if the Tribunal has given full reasons for its decision. In some cases (for example unfair dismissal cases, but not discrimination cases), the Tribunal can give its reasons in summary form. If you are thinking of appealing, you must write to the Tribunal Office to ask for full reasons within 21 days after the date on which the summary decision was sent to you. The period of 42 days for appealing to the Employment Appeal Tribunal then runs from the date stamped on the full written reasons.

Reviews

You can also ask the Tribunal to review its own decision. Tribunals have very wide powers of review, but you will need a good reason.

To apply for a review, you should write to the Tribunal Office asking for a review and stating why a review is appropriate. If the Chairman decides that the decision should be reviewed, then a date will be fixed for you and the respondent (or his representative) to go along and argue the point and call any relevant evidence.

Your letter asking for a review must be received at the Tribunal Office within 14 days from the date stamped on the Tribunal decision. The time limit can be extended, but this will be done only if there is a good reason for the delay.

You may wish to appeal if the review is unsuccessful. You should lodge your appeal to the Employment Appeal Tribunal well within the 42-day period and withdraw the appeal if you are successful at the review hearing.

Enforcing the decision

If you succeed in an unfair dismissal claim and the Tribunal orders the respondent to reinstate or re-engage you, you should write to the Tribunal Office asking for a further hearing if the respondent fails to comply. The Tribunal may then make an award of additional compensation or special compensation unless the employer can satisfy the Tribunal that it was not practicable to take you back.

Your Employment Rights

You should also ask for a further hearing if you succeed in a discrimination claim and the respondent fails to comply with a recommendation made by the Tribunal. Further compensation can be awarded (but subject to the overall maximum figure of £10,000) if the respondent unreasonably fails to comply with the recommendation.

What should you do if the respondent fails to pay any compensation which has been awarded to you? You should take the decision or a copy of it to your local County Court Office to arrange for the decision to be 'registered' in the County Court. A fee will be payable. Once the decision has been registered, it has the same effect as a County Court judgment. You can then try to recover the money by any of the usual methods, such as issuing a warrant of execution so as to send in the bailiffs. If you have any difficulty with the procedure for registering the decision or enforcing the judgment you should seek advice from a solicitor (under the green form scheme if you are of limited means) or at your Law Centre (if you have one locally) or at your local CAB.

CHAPTER 16
Other People's Rights Against You

So far, this book has been all about *your* rights. But other people have rights as well. If you ignore those rights you could be in trouble. You may lose your job. You may also have to pay compensation.

Your employer's rights

There are some rights which your employer has whether or not they are written into your contract of employment. These are some of the things which you must not do while still working for the employer:

- Damage your employer's property – deliberately or carelessly
- Secretly work for a competitor
- Do work on the side for your employer's customers
- Sell or give away confidential information.

If you do any of these things you could lose your job and your employer could also claim compensation from you.

You must also keep your side of the employment contract. You must do the things which you have agreed to do, unless your employer's behaviour is so unreasonable that the Courts will not hold you to the contract. The following are examples of promises to be found in many employment contracts:

- Not to take on a second job (moonlighting)
- Not to leave without giving a week's (or a month's) notice
- To work for a fixed period, such as three years.

In practice, many people leave without giving the proper notice and the employer does nothing about it. However, if your employer loses money because of your breach of contract a claim could be made against you. For example, you leave without giving the month's notice which is required and:

Your Employment Rights

- your employer misses an important contract deadline because of this; or
- your employer has to pay extra money to hire temporary staff.

In either of these cases you could end up having to pay compensation.

In your contract, you may have agreed not to do certain things after leaving your job. For example, many employees agree that they will not do any of the following things within, say, 12 months after leaving their job:

- Work for a competing business in the same area
- Approach, or accept work from, the employer's customers
- Poach any of their former employer's other employees.

Your former employer could go to the Court to ask for an Order to stop you doing any of these things. You will, however, be able to fight the case if the restrictions were unreasonable. This kind of restriction is to be found in contracts of all kinds. You may be a hairdresser's assistant who has agreed not to set up a rival business in the same part of town; or you may be a director of a large public company who has agreed not to go straight off to join the major competitor in Europe or Japan.

There are some things which you must not do when you leave a job, whatever your contract says. You must not:

- Hang on to your employer's property, including files and other documents
- Take copies of documents, like lists of customers
- Go through the files and make notes for your own use
- Sell or give away trade secrets, such as secret manufacturing processes
- Use trade secrets for your own business.

If you do any of these things your employer may be able to claim compensation. He may also be able to get an Order from the Court to stop you profiting from what you have done.

Your fellow employees' rights

Your fellow employees at work also have rights against you. For example, if someone is injured he or she could have a claim against you if you have caused the injury by:

Other People's Rights Against You

- Any kind of horseplay, such as pushing him or her or throwing things about
- Leaving dangerous equipment unguarded
- Driving a fork-lift truck without paying attention
- Causing a dangerous obstruction.

In all these cases you could face a claim for compensation. You could also face disciplinary action and in a serious case may even lose your job.

You could be in really big trouble if you deliberately do something to injure a fellow employee. The following are examples of things which you must not do to other employees:

- Beat them up or hit them
- Indecently assault them
- Sexually harass them in any other way
- Subject them to racial abuse.

Remember that the law forbids sexual and racial harassment even when no physical contact is involved. You could face a claim for compensation. You could also lose your job. You could also, in a bad case, end up in the dock facing criminal charges.

Customers' rights

Customers also have most of the rights which your fellow employees have. A customer could bring a claim for compensation against you for

- Injury caused by your carelessness
- Damage to property caused by your carelessness
- Any kind of assault
- Racial discrimination
- Sex discrimination.

Remember that the price of doing any of these things could be a very high one, particularly where you have done something deliberately. You may have to pay compensation, you may lose your job and you may even face criminal charges.

Index

Additional award 65-6
  increased amount of for discriminatory dismissal 67
Aircraft 7
Ante-natal care, time off for 39

Basic award 64
  minimum amount of in trade union related dismissal cases 88

Commission for Racial Equality 13, 18, 53, 96-7
Compensation for injured feelings 17, 65, 67, 76-7, 86
Compensatory award 64
Constructive dismissal 72-7
Continuous employment 57, 59
Contributory fault 66

Deductions from pay 21-2
Direct discrimination 11-12, 49-50
Disabled employees 18-19

Employees, meaning of 7
Employment agencies 17
Equal Opportunities Commission 13, 18, 53, 96
Equal value, meaning of 46

Genuine occupational qualification exception 14-15
Guaranteed pay 24-5

Illegal contracts 9
Indirect discrimination, meaning of 13-14, 51-2
  usually no compensation for 13-14, 52, 68
Insolvency of employer 25, 68, 84
Interim relief 89, 99-100

Job evaluation 46-47

Laid off, rights when 23-4
Like work, meaning of 46

Material factor defence 47
Maternity leave 35-7
Medical suspension pay 44

National security, as defence 16, 60
Northern Ireland 8
Notice, statutory requirements 56-7

Oil platforms 7
Overseas employment 7, 14, 22, 29, 35

Part-time employees 59, 80-81
Pensions 91-2
Police officers 16, 35
Positive discrimination 15-16
Pressure short of dismissal 89
Private households, jobs in 14, 81
Public duties, time off for 31-2

Questionnaire, in discrimination cases 12-13, 101

Racial harassment 51
Recoupment 65

111

Your Employment Rights

Redundancy pay, amount of 83
References 92-3
Religious discrimination 8
Resignation 71-2

Safety officers, time off for 32
Same employment, meaning of 45-6
Scotland 50-51, 98, 109
Sexual harassment 50-51, 98, 109
Share fishermen, meaning of 81
Ships 7
Short-time working 23-4
Special award 65-6, 88
Statement of contract terms 28-9
Statutory maternity pay 37-9

Statutory sick pay 41-2

Time limits 9, 17-18, 97-8
Trade unions, discrimination by 16-17
Trade union membership 16-17, 61, 87-9
Transfer of business 57

Unfair dismissal 55, 59-66

Variation of contract 28, 72-5
Victimisation 11-12, 14, 52-3, 67
Wage reduction 22-3, 72
Wrongful dismissal 55, 56-9